Wade's work in communication theory is a must read for survivors, institutional leaders, and everyone. In a powerful, easy-to-grasp book, Wade distills the strategies and communication tools abusers use to manipulate, abuse, and resist accountability and transparency. Understanding these dynamics empowers survivors to recognize and name what they have experienced and empowers all of us to identify and stand against abusers and abusive organizations. Reading this book and evaluating leaders and ministries with this knowledge will change you forever, for the better.

RACHAEL DENHOLLANDER, speaker, victim advocate, and author of *What Is a Girl Worth?: My Story of Breaking the Silence and Exposing the Truth about Larry Nassar and USA Gymnastics*

Something's Not Right is a beacon of truth and wisdom for the abused and a help in their healing. It is a warning about power mismanagement as well as a guide for eradicating evil from our churches. Wade Mullen's expertise provides a window into the insidious language of abuse and impression-management strategies so often present among church leaders.

SCOT McKNIGHT AND LAURA BARRINGER, authors of *A Church Called Tov: Forming a Goodness Culture That Resists Abuses of Power and Promotes Healing*

Something's Not Right is essential reading for every leader. Wade Mullen brilliantly unpacks the game plan organizations often use to manage their image in a crisis

and to self-preserve at all costs. This book will change the way you see and think about abuse forever.

STEVE CARTER, pastor and author of *This Invitational Life: Risking Yourself to Align with God's Heartbeat for Humanity*

Wade Mullen has uniquely identified the hidden behaviors of abuse and has demystified the tactics used to hold victims in silent captivity. His research and voice have been an essential component of my own healing journey as well as a pathway forward in dealing with organizational dysfunction. His work is a useful tool for informative and transformative introspection for victims and organizations alike. This profound work offers a path toward authentic forgiveness, healing, and freedom.

VONDA DYER, survivor, advocate, and CCO of Minerva Consulting

Wade's work is essential reading for our growing understanding of toxic and abusive systems. His deep experience and profound insights will provide clarity for those who are confused and pave a pathway for a necessary reckoning and the ultimate healing we long for.

CHUCK DeGROAT, professor of pastoral care at Western Theological Seminary and author of *When Narcissism Comes to Church: Healing Your Community from Emotional and Spiritual Abuse*

In his book *Something's Not Right*, Wade Mullen brings insights, research-based knowledge, and clarity to the heavy topic of abuse. His years of work provide readers with a language that gives voice to those who have been silenced by abuse. He unpacks a vocabulary that can help individuals identify and articulate tactics abusers use. While he vulnerably shares his own journey of navigating abuse, he also provides a stunning picture of hope for the reconciliation and restoration that is always possible. This book is a must-read for those who have navigated abuse, anyone who helps survivors find healing, and leaders who steward churches and organizations that want to safeguard their cultures and systems from abuse.

KERI LADOUCEUR, pastor of Vineyard Christian Church, founder of New Ground Network, silence breaker, and survivor

I first met Wade Mullen where this book begins, during his first steps of a journey to understand and free himself from an abusive church and its leadership. In the time since, I've witnessed God's voice speaking through Wade to research, identify, and call out abusive systems and to advocate for victims and survivors.

Something's Not Right offers a balm for the abused, a platform to hear their stories, and a pathway for the church to stand by their side. If you are a victim of abuse, this book will identify the tactics of manipulation and misuse of power you have suffered from, giving you a language to name and confront that sin. If you are a pastor or Christian leader, your eyes will be opened to the overt and nuanced ways abusers sow deceit and doubt *in you*, co-opting you into silence (often unwittingly) at the very time victims need you to speak truth and be the comfort of Christ.

This book offers you a glossary to discern and steps to address the scourge of abuse.

JIM VAN YPEREN, founder and executive director of Metanoia Ministries, a nonprofit ministry serving churches in conflict

Wade Mullen is one of the most important voices in evangelicalism right now. His experience and research into Christian institutions and how they can and do enable abusers is vital reading for anyone who wants to be an advocate for survivors—or to gain an understanding of what makes so many of us culpable in protecting power. Mullen uses real stories, extensive research, and gentle truth telling to highlight what is possibly the most pressing issue facing the church today: How can we stop the epidemic of abuse within our sacred institutions?

D. L. MAYFIELD, author and neighbor

Mullen offers us a sincerely thoughtful, incredibly practical, and truly compassionate book on abusive systems and the consequences of cover-ups. Full of relatable examples and opportunities to tend to one's own pain from abusive systems while leaving room for self-evaluation, this book holds up an overdue mirror. Mullen vulnerably relates to the reader, offering us a glimpse into his own experiences with toxic leadership, and moreover equips us to recognize patterns of organizational abuse and what repentance actually looks like in such instances. I cannot recommend this accessible book strongly enough to anyone considering leadership in the church, society, or politics. I will be making it required reading for teams and organizations that I work with going forward.

CHRISTINA EDMONDSON, PhD, diversity strategy and team ethics consultant, instructor at Calvin University, and cohost of *Truth's Table* podcast

SOMETHING'S
NOT
RIGHT

SOMETHING'S NOT RIGHT

DECODING THE

HIDDEN TACTICS OF

ABUSE

AND FREEING YOURSELF

FROM ITS POWER

WADE MULLEN

TYNDALE
MOMENTUM®

The Tyndale nonfiction imprint

Visit Tyndale online at tyndale.com.

Visit Tyndale Momentum online at tyndalemomentum.com.

TYNDALE, Tyndale's quill logo, *Tyndale Momentum*, and the Tyndale Momentum logo are registered trademarks of Tyndale House Ministries. Tyndale Momentum is the nonfiction imprint of Tyndale House Publishers, Carol Stream, Illinois.

Something's Not Right: Decoding the Hidden Tactics of Abuse—and Freeing Yourself from Its Power

Designed by Jennifer Phelps

Published in association with the literary agency of WordServe Literary Group, www.wordserveliterary.com.

Scripture taken from the Holman Christian Standard Bible,® copyright © 1999, 2000, 2002, 2003, 2009 by Holman Bible Publishers. Used by permission. Holman Christian Standard Bible,® Holman CSB,® and HCSB® are federally registered trademarks of Holman Bible Publishers.

For information about special discounts for bulk purchases, please contact Tyndale House Publishers at csresponse@tyndale.com, or call 1-800-323-9400.

Library of Congress Cataloging-in-Publication Data

Names: Mullen, Wade, author.
Title: Something's not right : decoding the hidden tactics of abuse-and freeing yourself from its power / Wade Mullen.
Description: Carol Stream, Illinois : Tyndale Momentum, [2020] | Includes bibliographical references.
Identifiers: LCCN 2020021206 (print) | LCCN 2020021207 (ebook)
 | ISBN 9781496444707 (trade paperback) | ISBN 9781496444714
 (kindle edition) | ISBN 9781496444721 (epub) | ISBN 9781496444738 (epub)
Subjects: LCSH: Psychological abuse.
Classification: LCC RC569.5.P75 M85 2020 (print) | LCC RC569.5.P75 (ebook)
 | DDC 616.85/82—dc23
LC record available at https://lccn.loc.gov/2020021206
LC ebook record available at https://lccn.loc.gov/2020021207

Printed in the United States of America

26 25 24 23 22
7   6   5   4   3   2

I DEDICATE THIS BOOK TO
THOSE IN NEED OF
FREEDOM FROM ABUSE.
MAY THE THREADS THAT BIND
COME UNDONE.

CONTENTS

AUTHOR'S NOTE

The stories in this book were gathered in the course of my own experience, interactions, and academic research. Some are composites; all are based on true events. Names and exact details have been changed to protect the vulnerable.

FOREWORD

Something's not right. How many of us have had the uncomfortable awareness that something was amiss but had difficulty articulating exactly what was wrong? When we cannot find words to label what is awry, our discomfort may lead us to deny that a problem exists. In doing so, we risk an aftermath of self-blame: *Something was not okay, and I share the responsibility of having allowed it to happen.*

Dr. Wade Mullen is a trustworthy guide in such matters. He knows the way because he has been there. He knows that when something is not right there are often people who want us to think *we* are not right. They may seek to convince us that our thinking is off, our labels are wrong, or our imagination is running away from us. They may exclaim, "You need to trust us; we will fix it!" They may warn that we risk destroying the godly work that has been accomplished by giving voice to our concerns. Wade knows what it is like to be seen as a threat, to be silenced and pushed aside. He understands what it is like to have people authoritatively switch all the labels in order to cover up wrongdoing.

Having our experience negated is both disorienting and isolating. It is confusing. At times like this, we need courage. We need a map, and the signposts along the way need to be true.

Not only has Dr. Mullen been in this murky land himself, but for his doctoral dissertation he studied over one thousand cases of abuse in churches and the methods used by those institutions to cover it up, rename it, and deny it. He gives names to grooming techniques used by those who abuse their power. He exposes the silencing techniques used by individuals and systems to keep truth from coming to light or being believed. He brings to light the deceptions, the twisting of words, and the manipulations that silence people and shift blame to those who expose abuse as if they, and not the abuse, were the actual threat. Wade teaches us about impression management—tools and strategies for managing what others see. These tools have been used for centuries to confuse, mislead, and cover up actions and decisions that are destroying precious people created in the image of our God.

Knowing well that abuse silences others, Wade has stepped into the light and given voice to many silenced and wounded people. His signposts are clear and true. He understands the internal experience of confusion, the silenced voice, and the changing of labels such that bad is named "good" and good seems bad. He has gathered up his own painful experiences, wounds, and confusion, and through them he brings empathy and clarity to others. He calls things by their right names. This process often brings great grief because it entails seeing things as they are—as opposed to how we hoped they would be. Truth, however, also brings freedom. The light is on, our labels are correct, and we then move forward toward greater strength and the healing of wounds.

So read, listen, and apply these concepts—to yourself first, and then to those situations you face that are abusive, confusing, and hurtful. By reading and learning what Wade has to teach us, we will be safer for each other and carry a greater likeness of the one we follow, who said that he himself is both the Truth and our Refuge.

Diane Langberg, PhD
Psychologist

You think evil is going to
come into your houses
wearing big black boots.
It doesn't come like that.
Look at the language.
It begins in the language.

JOSEPH BRODSKY

SOMETHING'S NOT RIGHT

"This is abuse."

The words stopped me in my tracks. My wife and I had just finished recounting our story to some friends who had stopped by to check on us. They'd heard we were resigning from the church where I was youth pastor and were packing up to move, and they were worried about our family. They knew how much we loved the church and how committed we were to serving with integrity. But after hearing the details of our experience the past few years—the confusion, the secrets, the oppression—these words were their diagnosis.

I didn't want to believe them.

Nobody had sexually or physically harmed me. Other people in our community had suffered far worse. "Abuse" felt like a label reserved for them, for the blatant and violent experiences they had endured. I could think of a million reasons my situation wasn't like theirs.

And yet I couldn't deny what my wife and I had been through. I didn't know how to talk about it and didn't have the words to describe what I was feeling, but deep down I knew: *Something's not right.*

That night was a critical step in my journey toward freedom.

Recognizing the Language of Abuse

If you're like me, you may hear the word *abuse* and think, as I did, of physical or sexual harm done to another person. But the truth is, the term *abuse* is appropriate to far more situations than those. When someone treats you as an object they are willing to harm for their own benefit, abuse has occurred, and that person has become an abuser. Some of the worst forms of abuse are psychological. The victim may never be physically touched but nevertheless is traumatized by the experience of being emotionally manipulated and held captive by lies, threats, and neglect. A husband can control all the finances in a marriage and use that control to coerce his wife into compliance. This is financial abuse. A parent can destroy the self-image of a child through verbal attacks. Verbal abuse so often targets those who lack the means to withdraw or the power to advocate for themselves. In other words, abuse involves any action that takes power from another in an attempt to use them. And it almost always begins with language—words that lead to confusion and captivity.

This language is evil's greatest secret. Unknown to most, even its users, this language provides evil with its primary desire: power. It's a power acquired and retained through deception and used to harm and destroy lives. The language of abuse is, at its core, a collection of tactics for deception, and it allows the evil of abuse to spread. Because language is so important for abusers gaining power, and also for restoring power to those who have been abused, I use the terms *abuse* and *abuser* throughout this book, even though, as in my experience, it can be difficult to see your own situation that way at first.

Through my own experience of abuse at the church and through my academic studies, I became aware of a branch of sociology called "impression management." When I first discovered impression management research, I was shocked to find it wasn't more broadly available—and that it hadn't been widely applied to the various and ever-present scandals of our culture. Impression management tactics seemed to name the very ways that abusers gained their power in my life and in the stories I'd come across. My own research has focused on impression management in evangelical organizations, but the tactics are not unique to that context. I've collected and analyzed nearly one thousand cases of clergy abuse over the last five years to understand how abuse pervades these institutions. But the more I grow in my understanding of impression management tactics, the more I see how these same tactics are used by abusers of all kinds, to perpetuate all types of abuse. The tactics of impression management used by organizations to cover up their wrongs are the same tactics used every day by abusers throughout the world—and that have been used by evil powers throughout history. There is a pattern that accompanies abuse, as if abusers are somehow reading from the same playbook.

If we can learn to decode these evil tactics—if we can *learn the language of abuse*—we can stop the cycle: we can make abusers less effective at accomplishing destruction in our lives. The ability to identify and describe tactics that were previously unidentifiable and indescribable will restore the power that was taken from you.

Who This Book Is For

Maybe you still aren't sure whether the information in this book will apply to your situation or experience. Maybe the words *abuse* and *abuser* still feel harsh and extreme—words for what has happened to other people but not you. Maybe all you know is that something's not right, that something feels off when you think about a certain relationship or inter-action. That's okay. I wrote this book primarily for you. Even if you aren't sure whether what you're experiencing is abuse, I encourage you to keep reading. My hope is that by the end of the book, you'll have the insight, language, and direction you need to clarify your situation and take any necessary steps to personal freedom. Freedom comes first by under-standing, and understanding means having the language to identify and talk about your situation. I want to give you that more than anything.

If, however, you come to this book with a clear under-standing that the situation you find yourself in is, in fact, abusive, my hope is that these pages hold power for you as well. In being able to recognize, label, and describe the tactics of deception, you might be able to resist the ways in which such behaviors can be used to manipulate you. Understanding the tactics that have been used to coerce you is an integral part of the healing process. As you make sense of and gain the ability to describe what you've experienced, may you find the inner power to shine a light on these dark places of your story.

I've also written this book for those who are seeking to advocate for victims and survivors of abuse. I commend you for doing so and know how quickly others can condemn you for your efforts and question your motivation. I've been encouraged by the many advocates I've gotten to know. They sacrifice their time and energy to provide support, prevent abuse, and create a safer future. They speak truth to power for the sake of repair and redemption. They choose to side with the oppressed despite knowing it often will require standing in the dangerous position between the oppressed and their oppressors. It might mean remaining in that stance until the battle is won, requiring tremendous sacrifice, courage, hope, and faith.

I hope this book can also speak to those who are enabling abusers—either willfully or unknowingly. I hope your eyes are opened to see the abuser in your midst. That abuser might be a leader or an organization you have come to love and support. I understand how difficult it can be to acknowledge when people you love and respect turn out to be different than you thought, but it is necessary to understand the important role you play as a bystander. Abusive individuals and organizations might be using impression management tactics to hide what happens behind the scenes so their act can continue. You must recognize that it is not just those doing the hiding who are at fault but also those who benefit from the abuser's show and want it to continue. We might want to ignore what we see when just a portion of the curtain is pulled back, hoping that, through time or circumstance, the abuses will be resolved on their own. But organizations and their leaders are always faced with two choices when abuse happening on their watch comes to light: adopt truth telling and transparency, regardless of the impact on their approval, status, or image; or use the same tactics of abuse in an attempt to retain or regain legitimacy. This book will help you respond to exposure with truth telling by making you aware of tactics that might work against truth, justice, and compassion. Enabling abuse means allowing it the power it needs to control others.

When I was in the midst of my own abusive experience, I felt as if abusers had taken hold of the pen of my life's story. There were moments when I did not want to turn another page for fear of what the next paragraph or chapter might hold. I had lost control of my own story; it was in the hands of those who wanted to do me harm.

Perhaps that is your experience right now. If it is, I hope this book will give you the validation you need to know you are not in the wrong, you are not alone, and you deserve to be able to write your own story. I also hope this book will open your eyes. The best antidote to deception is truth. Silence grants evil exactly what it needs to be effective. Truth helps us speak what has been unspeakable, express what has been inexpressible, and articulate feelings for which we could not find the appropriate words. Truth helps us move from confusion to clarity and from captivity to freedom.

Something's *not* right. But by understanding the tactics of the abusers in your life, you can take back the pen and write your story anew.

CHAPTER 1

THE SHOW MUST GO ON

Some have compared getting truth out of an abuser to nailing Jell-O to a wall—if caught, they'll use any tactic necessary to wriggle free, to evade accusation, to save face, and to preserve their power and influence. By having a clear picture of the tactics abusers are likely to employ, we are less likely to be taken in by their practiced deception. This is why we must learn and understand the field of impression management research.

The best explanation I've read of impression management is from the late Canadian sociologist Erving Goffman, who defined it as the process of creating, influencing, or manipulating an image held by an audience.[1] Like Goffman, I find impression management best understood by using the

Impression management becomes unethical when the front-stage persona is used to hide truths that ought not to be hidden.

metaphor of a stage play: individuals (or organizations) are actors on a stage, and at any point, they are either behind the curtain or in front of the curtain. The play—what the audience sees—reflects the stage version of the actor. The actor strives to give the audience what they want, knowing that his relationship with the audience depends on it—that is the only way the show can continue. The audience reacts, and the actor adjusts his performance based on those reactions to keep the audience engaged.

The Show Must Go On

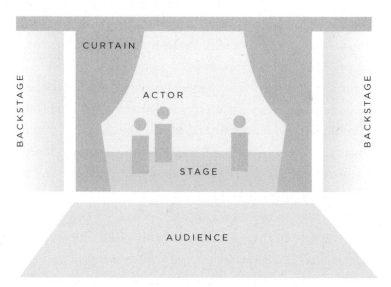

Abusive people and organizations try to manage our impressions through a series of tactics that will be described in this book. The effect is similar to the actors in a play managing what the audience sees and reacts to, which is different from what happens backstage.

Behind the curtain, however, is a different world. The audience can no longer see the actor. Behind the curtain, he can practice his performance, thinking of ways he can allure and appeal to the audience, developing who he is for the "front stage" act. The audience will never see this hidden side of him.

Now, the truth is we are all actors in our own lives, alternating between front-stage and backstage behavior as we go throughout our day. Our behavior in the privacy of our homes is different from our behavior in public. We change out of our pajamas before heading out the door in the morning, and the way we behave with clients is usually more professional than the way we relax at the end of the workday. Even certain rooms in our homes are kept cleaner than others just in case someone stops in for a visit. This is normal.

But the impression management becomes unethical when the front-stage persona is used to hide truths that ought not to be hidden. An abuser, for example, will use the tactics of impression management when grooming potential victims to conceal nefarious intent. An abuser or those seeking to protect the abuser might use the tactics of impression management to appear trustworthy while keeping the truth of the abuse behind the curtain or to explain the abuse away if the curtain is pulled back to reveal the backstage behavior.

Before we can learn the specific tactics of impression management as they relate to abuse—which we will explore in the coming chapters—we need to first consider what factors prime an environment for abuse.

Keeping Secrets

Gloria could feel her heart racing. Anxiety and fear always seemed to send her blood pumping before she was conscious that something was wrong. She wanted to walk out of the meeting. *Do I really need to do this?* she thought. *Maybe I'm making too much of it.* She took a deep breath and closed her eyes for a few seconds, as she had learned to do over the years, and she found herself easing back into a state of rest. *He may have done this to others,* she reminded herself. *And I can't keep carrying this secret.*

"So, how can we help you?" John asked. John was a board member and a vice president at the university. He was joined by the new head of human resources. Everyone knew John "handled" things at the university, and this meeting was no different. Gloria spent the next forty-five minutes telling the story of how a longtime professor had repeatedly made sexual advances toward her over the five years she had worked with him.

She was prepared to answer questions, but they didn't have any. She offered to share correspondence and other evidence, but John didn't feel it necessary. John suggested there might be some misunderstanding, alluded to the professor's outgoing personality, and assured her that it would be taken care of. Before she left, John mentioned how sensitive this information was and that she should keep it to herself for her own benefit.

Gloria didn't understand why they had seemed so

unmoved by her story. It made her feel as if she wasn't being heard or taken seriously. It was as if she was reading a story to someone who had heard it many times before. This was because they *had* heard it before, from multiple women who had recounted similar experiences.

Professor Simon was the university's most sought-after faculty member. He had been there long enough to have an academic building bear his name. Students were drawn to him. He made learning fun and seemed to come alive during a lecture. But his assistants knew a different side of him—an entitled and impatient person who always got his way. And some of the women came to learn that he even believed it was his right to claim them as his own.

But the powers above him needed his reputation to remain intact. If his backstage behaviors were exposed, it would shock the entire campus and community. They needed to keep this behind the curtain. They thought if they simply talked to Professor Simon, his behavior would change. But confronting him had the opposite effect. Talking without administering consequences made it clear to the professor that he could get away with his abusive behavior because the leadership would cover for him.

Little did Gloria know the walls within which she told her story were already plastered with secrets. The professor kept his abuse a secret from students, most colleagues, and the public. John and a few others at the top of the organization kept the reports a secret to maintain the university's reputation. And the women each kept their stories to themselves, thinking they were alone in their experience.

*   *   *

The chief desire of abusive individuals and organizations is to attain or retain power—most often the kind of power gained and held firm through deception. The person who abuses others feels the freedom to do so because of their power. And as their power grows, the individual or organization is free to abuse others with greater frequency and less resistance.

If power is maintained through deception, deception is maintained through secrecy. Abusers rely upon their ability to remain hidden. And, as we'll see, evil knows the best places to hide are those least likely to be searched and among people least likely to suspect abuse. Churches, as I have learned in my research, can easily become havens for abusers for these very reasons, yet we are still surprised when we discover abusers trying to crouch behind crosses and prowl among pews.

And nothing stays hidden without help. It takes others to keep a secret of abuse. Abusers often have to rely upon other people's cooperation to keep their show going. Just as most stage plays have a cast of actors, Goffman calls those who cooperate in the show "performance teams." Consciously or not, people end up working together to protect secrets, often by managing the flow of information. For example, organizations often try to save face after a scandal by overcommunicating some facts and undercommunicating others to the "audience." Whether the audience is the public, other members of the organization, the media, victims, or the civil authorities, the abuser and the performance teams around them omit or undercommunicate what Goffman calls "disruptive information," facts that threaten the audience's image of the abuser. At the same time, the abuser and performance teams selectively disclose information that improves the abuser's image. It's information control. All of the actors do what they can to keep the audience from gaining disruptive information that would redefine what they're seeing.

I sat in one meeting where senior leadership acknowledged numerous failures to the rest of the staff. They knew an employee had caused significant harm but did nothing to confront him or have him removed until the staff began writing letters to the board. The staff was upset with the entire senior leadership for enabling the abuse and looking the other way. The senior leadership called a meeting where they presented a catalog of wrongs, which looked like an act of tremendous transparency. They were thanked and applauded for it. But the most disruptive information—the facts that would have disclosed the full extent of the abuse—remained a secret. The audience's approval was based on a limited view of the situation. It was obscurity disguised as transparency.

Secrets can be potent in the right kind of environment, allowing deception to fester and evil to rule.

Most of us probably think we have a basic understanding

of what secrets are and how they function. In reality, their depth of power and breadth of function can make them incredibly complex. According to Goffman, there are five types of secrets: dark, strategic, inside, entrusted, and free.

Dark secrets—which we'll discuss throughout this book— are facts a person or an organization knows and conceals because if they were revealed, they could damage the image of that person or organization. Allegations of abuse, for example, are a common type of dark secret. Leaders of an organization may go to great lengths to hide an abuse allegation instead of reporting it because they know it would damage the organization's reputation. They want to be seen as a place where dark secrets do not exist.

Any secret that an organization keeps hidden to give it an upper hand in its dealings is a *strategic secret*. In this case, an organization might keep its plans for a merger with another organization a secret, knowing that such information might disrupt the merger if leaked. Strategic secrets allow an organization to be nimble and adjust for any type of response.

Inside secrets keep information between a small, tight-knit group within a larger body—for example, between a few close associates rather than an entire leadership team, or between a few friends planning a surprise birthday party for another friend. Inside secrets can include dark and strategic secrets but may also include secrets that would not be disruptive if leaked. Inside secrets involve being "in the know" and often come with a feeling of exclusivity. That in itself can be dangerous, so sometimes abusers will ask their victims to keep secrets as part of the grooming process, knowing that secret-keeping can be a shortcut to isolation. Even if inside secrets are not inherently dark, they can still be used in unethical ways. For example, many victims have found that their report of abuse to an organization was handled by a dedicated response team or kept within a small group of board members instead of shared with the entire board. (In Gloria's story at the start of this section, her report was kept as an inside secret with John and the human resources director and wasn't spread further.) Some abusive organizations create structures like this for the sole purpose of keeping certain secrets inside secrets, knowing that as the information reaches new people, the chances of that information becoming disruptive increases.

Similar to inside secrets, *entrusted secrets* aren't inherently dark. A secret is entrusted if the relationship calls for confidentiality. Information shared between a patient and a therapist or between close friends, for example, is usually an entrusted secret. Keeping these secrets is not necessarily wrong, although in some cases—like child abuse—the person entrusted with the secret might have a duty to report it.

Last, *free secrets* are those that do not threaten the image of the person holding the secret. The person who reveals information you entrusted to them might view it as a free secret instead of an entrusted secret—something to share with others for the thrill of gossip or to damage your reputation. To them, the secret is "free" because sharing doesn't cost them anything. Whistleblowers are often keepers of free secrets—while the information they have may be damaging to an organization, it is not damaging to themselves personally. This is why those who serve in advocacy roles must take great care to handle information carefully and with integrity.

These different kinds of secrets may seem like a purely academic distinction. But a greater understanding of and language for these abstract concepts is the beginning of your freedom journey. When you understand how abusers and their performance teams often defend cover-ups by claiming a need for confidentiality—masking a dark secret under the guise of another, more legitimate secret—you can begin to find your footing and speak clearly about your experience. An adult, for example, might claim confidentiality (*entrusted secret*) when confessing their addiction to child pornography to a pastor or counselor. And while that relationship might usually provide confidentiality, in this case (a *dark secret*), the pastor or counselor has an obligation to report it to the police—the claim to confidentiality is overruled by the need to protect children. Or an unethical business practice, such as tax evasion (a *dark secret*), might be treated instead as confidential information necessary to run the business (a *strategic secret*) or as an invitation to a junior partner to join the privileged ranks of those in the know (an *inside secret*).

Abusive situations are often covered up by treating dark secrets as another kind of secret—spreading responsibility to those who, even unwillingly, keep the secret because they do not feel free to share it without harming themselves.

Secrets are also a powerful factor in an abusive environment

Abusive situations are often covered up by treating dark secrets as another kind of secret.

because they can be used as tests of loyalty. I experienced the power of dark inside secrets while I was navigating the abusive culture of the church I worked for. Only certain board members—those who were closest to the senior pastor—were kept in the loop, while the other board members did not have access to all the information. This made it extremely difficult to work toward justice in the church and kept an abusive culture alive.

We must grasp the harm that is caused not just by abusers but also by those who fail to stop abuse and instead protect dark secrets. Our communities, schools, churches, and homes are safer when they are free of such secrets because victims no longer have to keep their stories hidden for fear of how they will be treated, either by abusers or by those who should be on their side. Instead, they are able to release their secrets and say to abusers and their enablers, "I am no longer yours." Each time we believe and advocate for victims, walls are broken down, truth is revealed, and hope is restored.

Sacred Roles

Steven seemed to relish the new position he had at the church. He immediately noticed people were calling him "Pastor Steve." At first it felt odd, but it grew on him, and soon he was referring to himself as "Pastor Steve" in correspondence and introductions. More and more people were asking him to pray at various functions, oversee ceremonies like weddings and funerals, dedicate children, and baptize new believers. His preaching also took on a new kind of bravado. It had a sort of swagger to it, as if the substance was in the style itself.

Some church members began to feel he was too domineering, but few could get away with offering recommendations or critiques. He walled himself off from criticism, and when criticism did make its way through to him, he felt blindsided and wondered why people weren't more assertive to begin with. He claimed his door was always open, but fewer and fewer people felt the freedom to approach him.

Most attributed it to his heavy workload and leadership style. Some found him confident and sure of himself. They liked having a leader who seemed in control. The truth was that he felt insecure but wanted to live up to his position at the church, so he ignored his inadequacies and acted qualified. Whenever a crisis unfolded, he quickly dismissed requests for outside assistance, concerned that asking for help would make him look incompetent.

He put all of his energy into his preaching and making the church as attractive as possible. As the church grew in numbers, his role grew in importance. People began to see him as the person God had placed in the community "for such a time as this." Eventually, Pastor Steve could not keep the stories of his domineering backstage behavior from getting out. By then the church felt they needed him. More than that, they needed the role he occupied and had transformed.

The role itself needed protecting if the church was to continue its growth.

*   *   *

The person who occupies a position of power—and the deference with which they are treated because of that position—is another important factor in creating an abusive environment. If we return to the analogy of the play, audience expectations affect how people in different roles are perceived. People in power learn to perform in a manner consistent with the role they have been given. In churches, for example, the roles of pastor, priest, preacher, and prophet often come with high expectations, one of which might be a supernatural calling. Those who occupy those roles, then, are not treated as ordinary people but as recipients of God's anointing, giving them implicit power over their congregants. We can see this in politics, too. When people censure the conduct of a politician or advocate for their impeachment, they argue that the politician has disgraced the *office*, not just himself or herself. The argument is that the politician should be held to a higher standard because of their role. I call these special positions "sacred roles" because they are invested with sanctity—they are seen as different, special, or set apart.

Yet it is precisely in the sanctity of these roles that the danger lies. Protecting a role's sanctity can become a motivation for hiding wrongs. The more leaders and their communities treasure these roles, the more they will see exposure as a threat, as a way to bring about disgrace to the role itself, threatening the role's (and even the community's) legitimacy. The greater the threat, the greater the likelihood of a cover-up. The role—not the community, not the victim, not even justice—is what must be preserved at all costs.

This kind of power and identity is tempting to those who struggle to sustain spiritual and emotional health. If a leader comes to a sacred role empty, narcissistic, and hungry, they'll likely feverishly quest for legitimacy and meaning, collecting audiences, platforms, awards, and luxuries to justify the position and their title. They begin to see people as objects to be manipulated, shaped, and molded to fit their own agenda and to further serve the role.

This isn't to say all sacred roles are exploited by abusive individuals. Despite the frequent news stories about scandals in churches and the political arena, there are still many pastors and politicians who serve with integrity and use their sacred roles for the good of others. Sacred roles are, however, vulnerable to abuse, especially when we are not aware of the warning signs. There are a few telltale symptoms to watch out for that can help protect sacred roles from being pirated by abusers.

First, the leader may insist on exercising their power in every scenario, even if they lack the expertise and resources necessary to be the decision-maker. Take, for example, the spiritual leader who, when faced with reports of child abuse in their congregation, chooses to handle the reports personally instead of involving law enforcement. Leaders can act as if they have the knowledge and skills to respond to an abusive

Just as a keystone holds
an entire arch in place,
so many of our organizations
are structured around a
keystone role, which makes
it difficult to entertain
removing leaders
who abuse their roles.

situation, but in reality most possess little experience or competency to respond appropriately. Instead, they act out of concern for their own role identity rather than out of concern for those who might be harmed by the abusive situation. Competency in one realm does not always transfer to competency in another, so it can be a warning sign when leaders in sacred roles try to exercise authority outside their usual sphere.

Another indicator of abuse of power within a sacred role is that the leader may appeal to their "anointing" or role to escape accountability for their own wrongs. I worked for one leader who constantly referenced his and others' qualifications. It became apparent that his greatest fear was being seen as unqualified for his role. He stopped at nothing in his quest for qualification, doing and saying whatever was necessary to avoid being seen as unqualified. At times, he and his supporters would simply appeal to his anointing. People were asked to believe that God had chosen him for the job and to respect God's choice. The sanctity we ascribe to leadership roles in churches and communities can be dangerous, but that danger is compounded when narcissistic leaders find their identity in the role and use it as a justification for domination.

Unfortunately, the final indicator of abuse within a sacred role extends to the people who surround and uphold it. Often organizations and communities that define these roles will join their leaders in their quest for qualification. The design of their system *requires* the leadership role as a keystone holding everything together. An orchestra needs a conductor. A plane won't take off without a pilot. Certain species, like giraffes, are key to the sustenance of an ecosystem. Just as a keystone holds an entire arch in place, so many of our organizations are structured around a keystone role, which makes it difficult to entertain removing leaders who abuse their roles. We come to depend on them to keep our organizations alive.

The danger of environments structured around sacred roles is this: communities need someone to fill their keystone roles, and narcissistic individuals eagerly search for opportunities to occupy them. We look for charismatic leaders who promise us a grand future. But once found, we often discover these leaders were looking for us before we were looking for them. We willingly provide them with the power they desire because they promise us something we want in return. And over time, narcissistic leaders slowly turn their organizations into monuments to themselves. The role becomes their identity, and success means proving through performance their right to occupy the role. Exposure, then, isn't just a threat to the role; it's a threat to who these leaders are. And for systems structured around keystone personalities, exposure threatens the entire system. So together, a narcissistic leader and a system that fuels and enables narcissism cooperate to maintain the performance to keep the structure intact. The show *must* go on.

Circling the Wagons

Jim had started his nonprofit to assist in global relief efforts. He presented a bold vision of ending hunger and developed an accessible way for people to get involved by packing their own basic foods and supplies. He and his wife enlisted three other couples they had known for a long time to serve as the board of directors. Ten years after starting, they were bringing in more than $10 million in annual revenue. In addition to Jim's making $400,000 per year in compensation, the nonprofit also paid Jim's wife an annual salary. Soon all three of their children were working as top executives.

And then Jim learned one of his sons had been accused of racial discrimination. Stories of his racist remarks and mistreatment of people of color began to emerge. Jim quickly called a meeting with his son and the board. Jim's son denied the accusations and claimed people were seeking to bring their family down. The board placed Jim's son on a leave of absence, hoping things would blow over. It worked. Six months later he was back on the job, and the few who complained had moved on.

A year later they were hit with a lawsuit. Jim's son had continued to mistreat people of color, and now the nonprofit was being accused of racial discrimination and negligence. The board held an emergency meeting. Jim was adamant that under no circumstances should they entertain the allegations against his son. "These people envy what we've built here and just want to see us suffer. I won't allow it." But Jim knew his son, and he knew the allegations were true. He had to choose between guarding the reputation of his family and firing his son, and in his mind, there was no debate. The reputation of his family would come first.

*   *   *

Another environment that can contribute to abuse is tribalism among the top executives in an organization. Tribalism can pervade businesses, nonprofits, high-control groups, and churches, especially if started or managed by close friends and family. This closeness heightens the tendency leadership might have to protect family members and friends when dark secrets come to light. In a tribal corporate culture, it's easy to justify compromises because of these close relationships. When faced with an image-threatening event, the tribe is more likely to cover up wrong in order to protect their own—to circle the wagons, as it were. They often choose to defend their image rather than confront the leader or protect the vulnerable.

The choices for leadership positions within a tribal culture thus become further calcified in a crisis—family members and close friends are chosen *because* they will be able to keep secrets (and have their secrets kept). The abusive organization will slowly shift more and more power to the top as a way to protect those most important to the tribe, and as the tribe becomes more protective of insiders, they become less trusting of outsiders, resulting in an even higher potential for abuse of authority.

This is a critical problem with a tribal system: concern for powerful tribe members and the effect a controversy will have on their image means the less powerful, who are often the most profoundly harmed, are forgotten and ignored. This is a key attribute of abusive communities and cultures—the most powerful benefit at the expense of the least powerful.

An indicator that a tribal culture has taken hold in an environment is what happens in a crisis: the leadership takes greater control of all decisions and communication, while assuring their audience that they have a legitimate claim to continued trust despite the power grab. It is a dangerous arrogance that keeps them blind to true problems and true solutions. And because tribal leaders tend to shun outsiders, they end up at a worse place than they were before the crisis: they have more power than ever but still lack a victim-centric, expert-informed understanding of the problem, increasing the potential for further crisis and abuse.

Nailing Jell-O

We've looked at the ways different environments can enable abuse through secrecy, sacred roles, and circling the wagons to protect close friends and family. The truth is, untangling environmental factors in abuse can be difficult and complex, and adding to the complexity is the shape-shifting nature of deception. Abusive individuals and organizations have likely practiced deception for some time. They've learned to keep secrets of all kinds hidden through various maneuvers, and over time they become masters at using deceptive tactics interchangeably depending on the audience and the circumstance. It's a flexible script that can be altered on the fly based on how others respond. As I said at the start of this chapter, accurately identifying and describing deception like this can be as difficult as nailing Jell-O to a wall. It is always easier for abusers to control others when truth remains elusive and confusion abounds, so it is in their interest to practice deception. In the absence of truth and discernment, an entire community can easily be deceived.

I say all this to reassure you: it's not your fault if you feel confused and overwhelmed at the prospect of untangling the web of abusive and impression management tactics. It is, by its nature, confusing and overwhelming. And while confronting abuse may sometimes seem unkind and unnecessarily disruptive, especially in the environments I described above, I must encourage you as well: if we ignore, minimize, justify, or excuse what we see to avoid disruption, then we help create space for deceivers to continue their charades—allowing their hearts to grow darker, the abuse to become serial, and more innocent people to be placed in harm's way. It is okay, and even ethical, to bring dark secrets into the light, provided the goal of exposure isn't to shame the abuser just for the sake of condemnation but to expose them as an act of mercy—for the abuser's future health and for the protection of others.

It may be daunting, but it is not impossible. As we unearth the most common tactics of abusive people and organizations in the pages you are about to read, I hope you find a new lens for understanding your situation. You are not crazy; you are not alone. You simply need new language for your experience, for with language, you can speak. And when you speak, you can regain what has been taken from you.

CHAPTER 1 SUMMARY

THE SHOW MUST GO ON

The behavior of many abusers is like a stage play: there are front-stage behaviors and backstage behaviors, and the two are often quite different. What happens on the stage is designed to appeal to the audience, hiding what happens behind the curtain. Three types of environments especially help to keep abusive backstage behavior from being discovered.

SECRETS

Five types of secrets—*dark*, *strategic*, *inside*, *entrusted*, and *free* (see pages 17–19)—help to keep abusers in power. Abusers will often hide dark secrets (like abusive behavior) behind another, more legitimate kind of secret.

SACRED ROLES

Environments where certain roles are viewed as special or sacred can be ripe for abuse, especially if those roles are necessary for the community to function ("keystone" roles).

INNER CIRCLE

Environments where those in leadership are closely connected in multiple ways (e.g., families or friends) can become abusive as those in power try to protect themselves instead of the vulnerable.

CHAPTER 2

CHARMS

If what Joseph Brodsky says is true and evil begins in the language, then evil language begins with charm. Great evil can wear the disguise of a kiss. It can invite you to explore its garden, only to release the trap hidden below the flowery surface once you've settled in. In the same way, charming words can be a pretext for abusive intentions. Excessive kindness can cover a hidden pit. Favors can camouflage a net.

Ingratiation through charms—flattery, favors, and alliances—exploits our desire for acceptance, our value of kindness, our acceptance of favors, and our occasional need for another's help. Few want to believe that stepping into what appears to promise them approval, success, or other benefits will result in the opposite, but as we look more closely, we begin to recognize how abusers play on our good intentions to draw us into an abusive snare.

Flattery

I was sitting at a restaurant with my brother on a hot summer day in a town hosting its annual car show. The place was over-flowing with customers, and the lone waitress was rushing from table to table trying to keep up. Both my brother and I noticed how her flustered appearance suddenly changed the moment she approached our table, replaced with a smile and charm while she took our order, only to change back again as soon as she left our table.

We've all been there: acting polite when serving others as a way of complying with expectations, even if we don't feel like it. Our waitress just wanted to earn a decent tip, so she hid her fluster and frustration behind a fake smile. It's a harmless—and perhaps even socially necessary—form of flattery.

Unfortunately, that's not always the case. When it comes to abusive individuals or organizations, flattery can be har-nessed to charm you into doing what they want. Flattery redirects your attention: by focusing on your real, fabricated, or exaggerated positive characteristics, you are kept from see-ing the true desires and agenda behind the compliments. Every person in my life that later showed themselves to be abusive and harmful to others was at some point exceedingly kind to me. The flatterer wants you to see something pleasant about yourself, not for the sake of encouragement or affirmation, but so that you think more highly of them.

Flattery can take the form of a simple lone compliment, a shower of praise, additional attention, a glance of affection, or a note of encouragement. The HBO documentary *Leaving Neverland* captures James Safechuck and Wade Robson recounting Michael Jackson's flattering behavior as a precursor to abuse.[1] They describe Jackson as an extremely kind, gentle, and generous person—one who made them feel good about themselves by encouraging their talents, expressing appreciation for their friendship, and lavishing them with gifts and unique experiences. But flattery can show up in simpler, more ordinary situations, like our interaction with the waitress: a coworker lauds your work in a meeting, going above and beyond to extol you in front of others; a romantic interest is relentless in their praise while on a date; a headhunter from another company begins their elevator pitch by noting how much potential you have and how you could really soar if you were in the right environment. Flattery works because it is close to the truth, a distortion of sincere kindness with dashes of exaggeration and untruths mixed into the compliment, making the deception extremely difficult to detect.

One common form of flattery is when someone tells you how exemplary you are. This exemplification makes you feel special, perhaps in ways nobody else has. Typically it is not just a simple highlighting of your attributes, but

Because we have
a natural tendency to
believe and accept what is
being said about us,
it is easy to be duped by the
deceptive tool of flattery.

a comparison with others in a way that declares you to be better than the rest. Exemplification can take myriad forms:

- "You are my favorite."
- "You are the cream of the crop."
- "You are the _____ person I have ever met."
- "You are the smartest person in the room."
- "There isn't a group of people I'd rather be leading."
- "You are world-class."
- "You are anointed."

When someone compliments us, we *want* to believe that what they're saying is true. And many times, what they say *is* sincere. But because we have a natural tendency to believe and accept what is being said about us, it is easy to be duped by the deceptive tool of flattery. One pastor in a church I studied as part of my research told his congregation they were "some of the most loving, generous, resilient people that any pastor has had the joy of leading and loving" and then later resigned in the wake of allegations of mistreatment.

An integral clue that a person is using flattery to coerce you is how they respond when their flattery isn't accepted or returned. Those most hungry for the praise of their support-ers might be most likely to flatter them, expecting that such excessive praise will not only be accepted but also returned. If it is returned—and it often is—it creates a cycle of flattery. The next time you're at a conference or speaking event, listen to how the speakers are introduced. If the emcee introduces speakers in a way that practically deifies them, they will likely begin their speech by returning the praise to the emcee with similar vigor.

As this wheel of worship spins faster and faster, and as flattery is embedded in the culture of a relationship or organization, it becomes increasingly difficult for anyone to interject a sincere expression of truth. This is why the more flattery you see from a person or within an organization, the more dangerous that person or organization might be. The constant praise creates blind spots as people are hesitant to speak criticism because flatterers begin to see criticism as negative, disruptive, and disrespectful. The ever-breeding flattery crowds out dissension, an important safeguard against corruption. Those who remain by an abuser's side tend to be those who are willing to insincerely praise their leader and unquestionably align themselves with their leader's agenda, often in hopes that they too might share in the power and adoration. It's a dangerous dynamic. Even if the primary leader is removed or replaced, a system built on this kind of flattery will simply install another narcissist to be the next keystone.

If you suspect someone is using the deception of flattery, you may not know how to go about confronting it. It can feel nearly impossible. With flattery, there's a power differential that looms over the situation, and you may feel controlled by it. What if you speak up and the flatterer becomes offended? Will the offense cost you benefits you might otherwise receive if you were to just play along? Maybe the flattery is so subtle and engrained in the culture, you doubt your own judgment. The truth is, flattery is just a single line from a script that tells a larger story. The abusive person will display multiple tactics of impression management—tactics we'll discuss at length in upcoming chapters—so it is best to see as much of the script as possible before seeking to interpret it and confront it. Your best defense is to know as much of the language of abuse as possible.

Favors

"I was hoping you could do me a favor," the senior pastor said. I was meeting with him one morning in his office.

I had come to expect such requests from time to time. Most were fairly painless. He was my boss, so I usually complied. But this time was different. He requested that I intervene in a crisis his family was going through. This made me uncomfortable because I felt like the favor crossed a line of professionalism. It was the first time I said no to a request, and I was afraid of how he might respond. The truth is, I felt this underlying fear each time I found myself on the receiving end of his many favors and requests for favors in return. Those fears would whisper,

- *What does he really want?*
- *What if I say no to his offer to help me?*
- *How will he respond if he discovers I suspect an ulterior motive?*

The request for a favor was powerful because of his own history of giving me gifts, doing me favors, and offering me his help. For example, I had asked for a modest raise after our second child was born. My request was denied. Instead, he told me to come to him with any financial needs I might have. The church had already provided us a home and was assisting with my education, which seemed to be a nice supplement to my low income. But I had accepted so much assistance that I was dependent on the pastor for my livelihood. It only seemed fair to do any favors he asked for.

Like flattery, favor behaviors appear—and even can be—innocent and harmless, but when they are used to control you, they create the potential for harm. The abuser who charms is a smuggler of fear. Deep below layers of flattery, gifts, and help lie messages of coercive power, whispering that noncompliance could result in harm instead of charm. In other words, the abuser smuggles fear in packages marked "Love."

Beneath the surface lies an unspoken expectation to do whatever is asked of you: the favors are used to control. And they can be powerful and alluring deceivers—they enhance your life, often in unexpected or unnecessary ways. It is normal to respond to a kind offer or gift with thankful appreciation. Who doesn't love a surprise help of some kind? The trick comes later, when the gift giver asks for a favor in return: the bank that contains all the favors you've received might cause you to feel forced to oblige, even if it's uncomfortable or not

The trick comes later,
when the gift giver asks
for a favor in return:
the bank that contains all
the favors you've received
might cause you to
feel forced to oblige.

really what you want. It's this robbing of choice that creates a dangerous power differential.

Abusers can also use their power to offer help in ways that are beyond necessary. This overhelping can be a form of manipulation in which you and others are made to believe that the only way you can succeed is with their help, which then makes you dependent upon them. Take, for example, an aspiring actress or musician who gets noticed by a celebrity who offers to coach them. Those offers of help might be a pretext to isolate and groom for abuse. Yet as the aspiring person benefits from the coaching, they begin to believe that they need that coaching in order to find success and are unable to move away from the abuser for fear of losing what they've gained.

Or consider Sarah's story. Sarah had started working in a congressman's office as a staff assistant. She had a passion for politics and hoped to one day become more involved in the legislative process. She didn't think much of it when the congressman asked her one day what her aspirations were. He was generally outgoing toward all the staff, but then he offered to take her "under his wing" and mentor her. "Your future is limitless," he told her. "I've never had someone work as hard as you. In some ways, I see myself in you when I was starting out." Sarah felt his high praise seemed a bit too much. After all, he really didn't know her all that well. But this was the kind of opportunity she was waiting for—a door was opening that would surely advance her career by leaps and bounds. Now, some fifteen years later, she looks back on her time working for the now-disgraced congressman and realizes that his offer to help was his way of getting closer to her.

Lifetime's explosive documentary on the survivors of R & B singer R. Kelly's abuse provides a demonstration of how powerful overhelping can be. Young girls were easily lured by R. Kelly with promises of succeeding in the music industry with his help. You can imagine how easy it would be for someone who dreams of becoming a musician like R. Kelly to receive his help when it is offered.[2]

As with most charms, favors as a deception tactic can be hard to distinguish from genuine offers of help. A hidden agenda to control or groom for abuse is often only revealed when you reject a request to return a favor or accept help. The favor renderer or overhelper might then remind you of past favors as a means of guilting you into compliance. They might also accuse you of betraying them, being unappreciative, or taking advantage of their kindness. These reveal that the initial favors probably were not genuine offers of help in the first place.

Alliances

"You and I have more in common than you think."

"It sounds like we both want the same thing."

"There is more we agree on than we disagree on."

Just as flattery and favors can be used to manage the impressions you are forming of another person, so too can alliances. When abusers seek to control your behavior by highlighting your commonalities, they are seeking to establish the appearance of an alliance. Like compliments and favors, not all attempts to form an alliance are inherently wrong. It makes sense in many situations to find common ground with others for the good of everyone involved. Abusers, however, exploit and misuse alliances, and there are some red flags you can look for.

An abuser might seek to form an alliance around real or invented shared experiences to exploit your vulnerability. Relationships ought to naturally develop on a continuum of intimacy, a wide-ranging spectrum in which people move toward each other as they develop their relationship. It takes time to develop trust. You wouldn't normally bare your soul to someone you just recently met. But an abusive person will often rush you through and over that natural process. We see this, for example, in situations with married child predators: they reveal very personal information about their marriages to their prey as a way to build trust and intimacy. Because of this rushed vulnerability, the victim is more likely to comply with the abuser's requests. For example, abusers who prey on kindhearted people might advertise their difficulties and hardships and then ask the victim for help. The victim feels the pressure to assist someone they have become so close to so fast. The abuser then praises the help they receive, which reinforces feelings of concern and a desire to keep helping.

This happens, of course, in everyday situations as well.

A person you agree to go on a date with might reveal some of the most painful moments of their life. You aren't sure how to react to such vulnerability and wonder if you should respond in kind. Rushed vulnerability gets you to share your own story and intimate details—creating an alliance of experience—and provides an abuser access to the deepest parts of your soul.

Similarly, abusers might forge an alliance around real or invented shared views. It is a potent tactic that exploits our desire for peace and agreement. I have often witnessed this in meetings and conversations where a person is challenged to defend their actions or views. Instead of responding to the challenge, the person will make comments that highlight subjects of agreement to distract from subjects of disagreement. You may bring up your concern about how some leaders are ignoring policies for the sake of pushing a certain agenda through or how certain standards aren't being followed. Rather than address these concerns, your boss may focus on how important the project is to the future success of the company. Your boss may go on to count up all the possible future benefits, and you find yourself unable to argue that this vision isn't compelling. Slowly but surely, criticisms are dropped and concerns assuaged by redirecting everyone to areas of shared beliefs or goals. Under the guise of alliances, abusers can disarm the threat to their control and power.

Another indicator of a deceptive alliance at work could be when an abusive leader or board attempts to control a crisis by insisting on one-on-one meetings with those they perceive to be a threat. What usually happens at these meetings? The leader may try to reiterate shared beliefs and goals. We're on the same team, remember? These meetings are often a trap designed to control your behavior and trick you into making statements of conformity that can later be used against you, as in Mason's story.

Mason had already moved on to another company, but he decided to report his abuse by his former supervisor after two years of keeping it to himself. He was asked to meet with representatives of the organization from human resources and legal. He had no idea the meeting was designed with the sole goal of reaching an agreement. They assured Mason that they were on the same page and that it would be in everyone's best interest if they could work together to find a solution. After a couple of meetings that appeared promising, Mason received a document that offered some monetary assistance for therapy and promises of reform. Mason, at this point, wanted to put the abuse behind him and trusted that the organization would have a safer culture in the future—which is all he really wanted. But years later, Mason found out there were other victims. He felt a compulsion to speak out but was bound by a non-disclosure clause tucked into the document he had signed. He never foresaw how that private meeting might one day be used to silence him. It pained him to hear the organization boast about how "pro-victim" they were despite having found a way to prevent him from telling his story. Adding to his pain was the sight of so many supporters of the organization who believed them when they would say things like, "We treat our employees like family." Yet he had never once heard from them since signing the document.

Why It Matters

Tactics of charm lead to devastating abuse, but the aftereffects are also long lasting for survivors. It's part of what's so disorienting and disillusioning about abuse: the realization that the kindness you once enjoyed and appreciated was actually a deception intended to harm you. Understandably after such a betrayal, it may be difficult to trust future displays of sincere kindness, to enter into genuine relationships, and to walk closely with another person. It is normal for people who have been abused by clergy—those who appear safe and who *should* be safe—to never want to enter a church again.

Again, though these ingratiating tactics of abusive individuals and organizations are not explicitly violent or in themselves harmful, if they go unnoticed or ignored, they actually make the community more vulnerable to further abuse. Ingratiating tactics appear, on the surface, to be positive displays of kindness, generosity, and friendship. Especially in cultures that place a high value on maintaining tact, avoiding disruptions, and believing the best about others, abusers can use these subtle tactics to repeatedly

Though these ingratiating
tactics are not explicitly violent
or in themselves harmful,
if they go unnoticed or ignored,
they actually make
the community more vulnerable
to further abuse.

cross boundaries without consequence, knowing they'll be overlooked.

Flattery, excessive attention, gifts, and kindnesses can groom whole groups of people to accept abusive situations. There are numerous cases in which entire communities have rallied to defend the character of an abuser on the basis of his or her kindness. I came across one case in my own research in which a revered youth pastor and school-teacher was accused of child molestation. The church and community held events to raise support for the accused, showed up at hearings, and purchased billboards to express their support. Meanwhile, the young victim and her family moved out of the neighborhood to escape harassment. The wave of support worked. He was even awarded Teacher of the Year. Fifteen years later he was convicted for the sexual abuse of seven children. In more recent cases, this display of community support is seen in social media posts where supporters claim the accused could not be guilty because of how generous they know the accused to be. In cases like these, the very behaviors used to groom someone for abuse are offered as evidence of innocence.

In order to see how charms can prepare you for abuse, imagine the following scenario: a man sits down next to you in a coffee shop while you are reading a book. He engages you in conversation and asks you what you are reading. His behavior seems a bit intrusive, but he appears innocent enough, so you tell him it's a novel about a newlywed American couple who decide to live "off the grid" for an entire year. He volunteers a story of his own experience hiking the Adirondack Trail. "You should try it someday," he finishes. "I'd be happy to talk you through what I learned if you ever want to give it a go." At this point you are not sure how the conversation led to such an offer. You respond with a simple, "Thank you. I'll keep that in mind."

As you return to your book, he settles in and starts watching a movie without earphones. A few minutes in, it's clear others are annoyed—there are lots of side-eye glances, and you can hear passive-aggressive huffing from several others—and though you think about saying something, you choose instead to ignore the behavior to maintain order and peace. Maybe you do not want to create a scene. After all, you did just have a friendly conversation. Perhaps you fear a negative response. Or maybe you think this behavior can't last forever—either you'll leave or he will. Whatever the reason, you and the others in the coffee shop say nothing as if you cannot hear the movie or are not bothered by it.

A few weeks later, you find yourself back in the coffee shop, and the same man walks in and sits next to you. *Not again*, you think. He strikes up some more conversation, throws in a few compliments, and then begins watching his earbuds-free movie, but this time you notice the volume is louder than before.

What has happened? Since nobody said anything during prior visits, the man feels confident: he has learned what he can get away with, and now he can cite past precedent if someone objects to his behavior. "I did it before," you can picture him saying with a winning smile, "and no one complained." Knowingly or not, the community has worked together to redefine boundaries that communicate which behaviors are tolerated and which are confronted.

Erving Goffman used the term *tactful inattention* to describe a phenomenon in which everyone works together to maintain order despite the existence of questionable behaviors, knowing that speaking up will likely cause disruption.[3]

The coffee shop example is a fairly harmless, albeit annoying, situation. But now consider how tactful inattention can aid abusers.

Abusive people, like the man in the coffee shop, will test boundaries to discover what can be done without objection. They often use charms to win people's favor and trust, and then they exploit that trust by crossing boundaries—boundaries that would ordinarily be met with resistance if that trust were not present. It is exactly that trust gained through charms that allows them to further their abuse to more extreme and violent behavior.

Not all kindnesses are harmful or tactics of abuse. But it is because charms are so hard to detect that they are often the dangerous camouflage for abuse.

CHAPTER 2 SUMMARY

CHARMS

Charms are behaviors designed to groom others for abuse. Ingratiating behaviors such as flattery, favors, and alliances make recipients feel good about themselves, but they can serve as a cloak for abusers.

FLATTERY

Flattery focuses your attention on your real, fabricated, or exaggerated positive characteristics—and distracts from the true desires or agendas behind the compliment.

FAVORS

Favors—such as gifts or offers of help—when used by abusers, can put you in a position where you feel indebted and obligated to the other person and more likely to comply with their desires.

ALLIANCES

Alliances create common ground between you and an abuser that can make you more willing to go along with and less likely to report abusive behavior.

CHAPTER 3

DISMANTLING YOUR INTERNAL WORLD

My wife and I would often discuss how the leadership at the church looked down on me. I was the young and impulsive idealist who didn't understand life's realities. So when I reported abuse, I was referred to as a "letter of the law" kind of person with a sensitive conscience. When I later advocated for better policies to protect children and youth and for more accountability for the senior pastor who didn't report abuse, the leadership said I was overreacting and just needed to get things off my chest. Meeting after meeting, I was told I was confused, harboring a root of bitterness, and disrespecting authority.

Throughout the years I served under their leadership,

they tried to control me numerous times by dismantling my sense of self. When my wife tells people our story, she often mentions how defeated I seemed after coming home from meetings with the leadership. This dismantling of my internal world left me questioning my beliefs, doubting my emotions, and searching for my identity.

If charms are designed to create a false sense of trust with the victim, dismantling tactics are designed to destroy the victim's external and internal worlds, keeping them in the web of abuse the abuser has spun. Dismantling tactics are, most clearly, attempts to control a targeted person through actions involving intimidation, humiliation, and outright violence to produce feelings of fear and shame. Think of the intimidating roar of a lion. If you've ever heard a lion's roar up close, you know the fear it can produce. That fear—both in the case of the lion and in cases of abuse— keeps us frozen and unable to escape the danger or even call for help.

For this reason, I encourage you to read this chapter with care and caution: the descriptions and commentary around each dismantling tactic might recall painful memories and emotions. Especially if you're reading this book as an abuse survivor, it's important to take breaks for your emotional health. Dismantling tactics are, at their core, assaults on beauty, on the image of who God has created you to be. There is no shame in attending to what you need, and it is important to honor your journey, if you need to, by disengaging from this material for a time as a form of self-care. Come back to it when you're ready. But do come back to it if you can, for you will be better equipped to protect beauty when you learn how, when, and why it is sometimes dismantled. Remember, knowledge is the foundation for reclaiming the power that has been stolen from you.

Identity

Trauma expert Diane Langberg points out that the word *trauma* comes from the root *trau*, meaning to turn, twist, or pierce. Isn't that exactly how it feels when an abuser dismantles our inner world? Everything is a little twisted, turned around to the point where we're not sure what reality is anymore. By getting us to distrust our own minds, the abuser bends trust away from what is trustworthy and toward the abuser. Fran Widmer, a trauma survivor and developer of child protection policies, said, "There is not a single place within [an abuse victim] where the impact [of trauma] is not comprehensive and all-encompassing. If you take a tour into their life, you will find nothing but ruins. Ruins that need excavating in order to find even a speck of life remaining."[1]

Nothing but ruins. The abusive person dismantles the internal world of the victim until nothing of substance remains. How do they accomplish such a travesty? They often begin with the victim's own sense of identity.

We can see this dismantling tactic in Sarah's story. Sarah was fourteen when a friend invited her to a church youth

The abusive person dismantles the victim's internal world until nothing of substance remains. They often begin with the victim's own sense of identity.

group event at a local fundamentalist church. She spent most of her evenings at home bored and thought a night with some of her peers couldn't be much worse. So she went, and then she kept attending. A year later, she was baptized during a summer church service. She joined a Bible study with other teenage girls, where the leaders taught her the need to be separate from the "world," protect her purity, and become a biblical woman. She was told not to watch movies or listen to secular music. She became increasingly disconnected from her family and allowed nonchurch friendships to dissipate. An older woman took her shopping to buy modest clothing and warned her of being a "stumbling block" to men. She started noticing how men occupied all the prominent roles in the church and how women and children were treated as second-class citizens.

Now, as an adult, she describes her experience at the church like walking into a large house and becoming a slightly different person with each new room she entered— then finding that each door had been locked behind her. A piece of her identity fell off with each step she took into the culture of the church, pieces that were quickly replaced with ones that matched the church's values until she became one of them.

Our own identity is slowly stripped away when an abusive person or organization engages in the process of exchanging our culture, values, beliefs, name, belongings, preferences, and desires with a ready-made identity manufactured by the abuser. Something as seemingly innocent as giving you a nickname is a prime example of this kind of attack, a form of control that replaces your given name with a name chosen by the abuser. You've likely encountered this without a passing thought because, unfortunately, nicknaming is part of our culture: the big guy on the team is "Tank," the smallest is "Pipsqueak" or "Runt," and the most studious in the class is addressed as simply "Nerd." I've witnessed powerful men call women they've just met "sweetheart" or "honey," romanticizing them without really knowing them. It may seem harmless, but in truth, given names are important anchors to our sense of identity. Of course, those who honor your identity can, at times, use nicknames in a harmless and endearing way. However, exchanging that name with another without honoring your agency can be demoralizing, an act that strips you of the identity captured in your chosen name. Unfortunately, children and other marginalized groups are the most common targets of nicknames.

We see this naming operating at a societal and institutional level as well. Just watch the political ads in an election season. Politicians use belittling and pejorative names to shape people's perceptions of their opponents. Even preachers have demeaned entire groups of people from the pulpit. When left unchallenged and uncorrected—or worse, when met with laughter (a key indicator that humiliation is taking place)—people are primed to more readily accept similar attacks from those in their lives who have been conditioned to see them as occupying a lower status. As we talked about in the last chapter, once a boundary is crossed, it becomes easier for abusers to justify going even further.

But the dismantling of our identity doesn't stop with our names: our identities lie even in our possessions. Jews who were placed in ghettos by Nazis during World War II had all of their belongings confiscated and were given a new form of identification. Children were separated from their parents. Families were torn apart. You might experience this if you enter into a relationship with a person who starts controlling what you wear, buy, and enjoy. They might belittle your hobbies and shame you for being interested in certain activities. People and artifacts that fill our lives shape who we are and help define our identity. The dismantling of our identity seeks to leave us dispossessed of what we value most.

It is very difficult to be reduced to a simple category of another person's making. By being labeled and stripped of all that makes you *you*, it becomes even more difficult to confront the lies and fight for your worth.

Self-Respect

As your identity becomes increasingly dismantled, it becomes easier and easier for the abuser to then target your self-respect. A person who believes they have the right to redefine you will also feel the freedom to humiliate you. And since the definition of who you are is no longer yours alone to control, self-respect quickly erodes. Like using nicknames, humiliation through teasing and bullying language is key to dismantling your interior life because it causes you to question not only your identity but also your inherent worth.

We can see this in what happened in Micah's friendship with Harris. The first time Micah felt wounded by his new friend Harris was when they were playing basketball together. Harris jokingly referred to Micah as "Slingshot" because of the awkward form Micah used when shooting the basketball. Micah laughed along at first, but then Harris started calling him "Slingshot" whenever they were hanging out with the rest of the team. It was clear Harris enjoyed the laughter produced by the nickname he came up with. During practice, other guys would yell "Slingshot" each time Micah took a shot. It didn't take long before he saw his play suffer. He lost his confidence, and within a year he gave up the sport altogether. An activity that had shaped him and defined him in positive ways had become a source of woundedness and shame.

You can see the same effect in communities run by tyrannical leaders. These leaders commonly humiliate people in public. One victim of childhood clergy abuse described the way the abusive pastor would humiliate people from the pulpit. The church kept the children fearful of acting out, even hanging a paddle in a prominent place for them to see. Humiliation like this is used as a means to control others.

But like many facets of abuse, humiliation doesn't have to be public to be damaging. Take, for example, the employee who cannot receive the basic resources needed to do their job—like a simple budget—without asking the manager for permission. The manager forces the employee into an arrangement in which they have to ask for help whenever they need something. It's subtle, but what the manager is doing is controlling the employee by controlling the resources they need to sustain themselves. *"It's for your own good,"* the manager might say. *"I just want you to succeed."* But if the employee is perfectly capable of providing for their own needs and is forced to rely on another to meet those needs and to make every decision, humiliation is the obvious result.

Dismantling your self-respect can even happen without your knowledge. This is best represented through an invasion of your privacy. For example, a sexual abuse survivor who was forced to perform on camera does not have control over who is observing them for sexual gratification when the video is posted. Survivors who were used for the production of child sexual abuse imagery describe the humiliation of knowing their images are public. Unfortunately, this particular form of assault on self-respect seems to be on the rise as technology becomes more advanced. From installing hidden cameras in bathrooms to secretly taking pictures with smartphones or sharing photos or other material that was intended to be private, the abuser violates your privacy, dismantling the most essential of boundaries without your knowledge of the unwanted intrusion.

Dismantling Agency

Some of the most common, and hurtful, responses survivors hear when they tell their story of abuse are "Why didn't you just say no?" or "Why did you stay in the relationship for so long?" or "Why didn't you just quit your job?" These questions reveal a lack of understanding of how an abuser traps a victim by slowly dismantling their agency—their ability to choose for themselves.

As the abuser constructs a new world with a newly defined reality, they dictate and control actions with increasing scrutiny and highly invasive rules. A fundamentalist church in North Carolina is infamous for its stringent rules. Members are reportedly expected to follow dozens of rules that include smiling whenever the pastor commands them, receiving permission before buying a home, and refraining from listening to the radio. We see clear examples of this dismantling of agency in high-control groups, popularly called "cults," but it also shows up in interpersonal relationships. Abusive friendships develop when one person starts imposing rules on the other—telling them what they can and cannot do. An autocratic husband and father limits the freedom of his wife and children through highly defined roles. Those in abusive situations are often subjected to a dizzying set of rules. In many cases, the victimized individuals are not even aware of all the rules until they break them or are put in a situation where they need to agree to them.

Some signs you might be in such a relationship are if you find yourself in constant trouble for not meeting expectations that were not communicated or that you did not agree to, if you feel as if you are always looking over your shoulder or "walking on eggshells," and if you feel persistent anxiety that comes with living under the ever-present but unpredictable storm cloud of condemnation and punishment. It can be hard to extricate yourself from such a situation because the rules do not allow for it, and breaking the rules results in abusive, and sometimes life-threatening, retaliation.

Hope in the Ruins

If you find your interior world being dismantled in these ways but the abuser has robbed you of your ability to fight back, then what recourse do you have? Where can you find hope?

If this has been your experience, then I encourage you to talk about it. Seek out a safe way to tell a professional or someone in a position to help you. You may not know what to say, but that's okay. One of the reasons telling our stories of abuse can be so daunting, and so fragmented at times in their expression, is because we are trying to piece together the parts of us that have been dismantled, like giving a tour of ruins and trying to remember what once stood there. It is another consequence of the abuser's destruction. Even if you do not have any words to describe what happened

One of the reasons
==telling our stories of abuse==
can be so daunting
is because we are trying
to piece together
the parts of us that
have been dismantled.

to you, you can simply say, "Something's not right." And perhaps the person you tell can validate your experience, bring clarity to confusion, and support you as you take steps toward freedom.

If you don't think you can tell another person, then tell yourself. Take an inventory of your experiences. Ask, *Where have I experienced lies? What has caused hurt? What has made me angry? When have I felt humiliated? Where do I feel unnecessary limitations, perhaps unspoken expectations, constricting me? Do I feel like I can stand up for myself? Why not? What do I think might happen if I begin to assert myself?* These kinds of questions can help you answer a question every deceptive abuser despises: *What is true?* This can be a surprisingly painful experience, but let that pain speak to you—it may be a voice of truth—and the sooner you see what the abuser hopes you are blind to, the more hope there is of freeing yourself from the abuser's snare. Until you know what is true, it will be difficult to know what to do. The ingredients of trauma include confusion and captivity. Freedom from trauma, therefore, requires truth and empowerment.

CHAPTER 3 SUMMARY

DISMANTLING YOUR INTERNAL WORLD

Abusers groom others for abuse through dismantling their internal and external worlds. Dismantling your internal world is an assault on who you are—on your identity, self-respect, and agency.

IDENTITY

An assault on your identity seeks to distance you from what makes you *you*—your culture, values, beliefs, belongings, preferences, even your name—in order to replace it with a ready-made identity of the abuser's choosing.

SELF-RESPECT

An assault on your self-respect uses tactics like humiliation to destroy your dignity and self-worth.

AGENCY

An assault on your agency removes your ability to choose, usually through the abuser imposing rules that you may or may not have agreed to. It is accompanied by anxiety that you might be punished for not complying.

CHAPTER 4

DISMANTLING YOUR EXTERNAL WORLD

Dismantling tactics don't stop at a victim's internal landscape. Abusers systematically and simultaneously begin demolishing a victim's reality through attacking the support systems that keep them connected to what is true and empowering. To dissuade the victim from trusting anyone else, abusers lace every conversation with deceptive messages:

- "They don't really care about you."
- "Why do you listen to them?"
- "You don't need them."

Any person or group of people that might see through the abuser's deception, or otherwise advocate for the victim, becomes a threat to the abuser. Isolation is key to the success of abuse: as victims are severed from sources of external help, the abuser ensures that, should the victims ever decide to confront the abuser or appeal for help, no one will be there to hear their call.

Abusers will seek to dismantle your connection to supportive relationships, institutions, and sources of understanding in their attempts to isolate you.

Supportive Relationships

When Brad's wife, Jessica, asked to go to therapy, he exploded. After Brad refused to get help for their marriage, Jessica decided to meet with a therapist on her own. That's when things really started to get bad. Feeling threatened, Brad told her that a therapist couldn't help her, that she was overreacting, and that they couldn't afford any new bills. In reality, he worried that he would lose control over his wife if she went to a therapist. So he constructed an explanation that made her feel terrible about herself: how embarrassing, how shameful, how *weak* that she couldn't solve her problems on her own. What could the therapist tell her that he couldn't? If only she would actually listen to him. Plus, what would people think about them—about their marriage— if they knew she was going to therapy? Before long, Jessica canceled her appointments, deluged and defeated by these twisted arguments, convinced that her husband was the only support and authority she needed.

Abusers who charm
and dismantle you as
a means of control
will become paranoid
that their schemes
might be exposed.

Abusers who charm and dismantle you as a means of control will become paranoid that their schemes might be exposed. They fear losing control. As the relationship becomes increasingly coercive, the abusive person will try to prevent your empowerment and their exposure by cutting you off from supportive relationships like family, friends, or even those who offer help in a professional capacity, like therapists. They might try to convince you that limiting your ties to other relationships is for your own protection, implying that putting too much trust in other people would be risky. However, if this results in secrecy, isolation, disempowerment, and imposing unwanted limitations, then the arrangement is for their protection, not yours.

Institutional Support

In addition to isolating you from supportive family and friends, an abuser will work vehemently to dismantle your belief in institutional support that could rescue you from the abuse. Investigative journalists represent one institutional support that is often stigmatized by abusive individuals and organizations. I've been called into board meetings where I've been warned of getting too close to the media. I was told these people are just looking for "hit jobs" and would twist whatever I said to serve their agenda. Instead of relying on journalists to be governed by the ethics of their profession, abusers might repeat the continual threat of misrepresentation: "Whatever you say could be used against you."

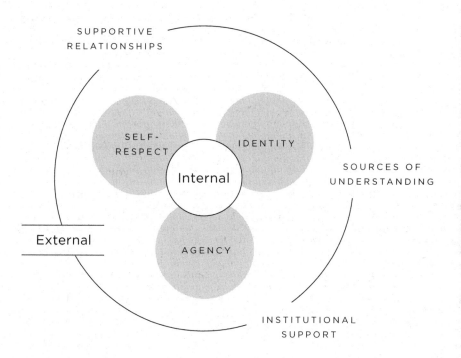

Dismantling Your World

Your internal world consists of the private, often hidden, areas of your life you typically only share with those you trust—emotions, beliefs, hopes, memories, and so on. Your external world is made up of the public, not-so-easily-hidden areas of your life typically experienced by others—family members, teachers, coaches, colleagues, therapists, etc. In an ideal environment, your connections to the external world can serve as healthy supports to your internal world, and together they form a tapestry of your unique and special life. In an abusive environment, the external world is dismantled in order to gain easier access to your inner world, which the abuser also seeks to dismantle.

The truth, of course, is that journalists have always played a critical role in society, helping the public discover important truths that oppressors have kept hidden. Many of the worst abuses throughout history would have continued in secret were it not for the work of investigative journalists. But because of this truth telling, they present a great threat to the world and work of an abuser, and therefore, abusers might work to dismantle their credibility in your eyes.

I've seen this dismantling in organizational settings where employees who feel they've been mistreated by a supervisor are told by the supervisor that going to HR will only make things worse. I've seen it in boardrooms where a decision to hire outside professionals to investigate violations is hijacked by a board bully. In each case, the abusive manager was seeking to protect their control of the situation.

Similarly, abusive organizations—and often those affiliated with Christian communities, using Bible passages like Matthew 18 or 1 Corinthians 6—work to dismantle and attack the reputation of the American legal system. The judicial system is said to be adversarial, pitting people against one another and causing further separation instead of reconciliation. People come to view the courts as places to avoid instead of places to find justice. Sometimes abusive organizations use their own policies and procedures to eliminate the threat the legal system poses. In my experience at the church, the leaders who employed me eventually brought in Christian conciliators to handle our dispute (and later my resignation) after I continued to report abuse. In order to participate, however, I had to agree to keep everything in our mediation confidential and had no say in who the conciliation organization was. Later, I discovered the lawyer who provided legal assistance to the church was the director of the organization that created the rules of conciliation I was being asked to agree to. When I declined to participate, I was told I needed to "follow biblical principles." It was as if the church leaders were saying, "We are God's agents. We know God's will for you. If you don't comply, you will be acting against the will of God." While this tactic was shocking to me at the time, I've since come to learn that this all-too-common practice is established to prevent a member of the organization from pursuing legal action.

We should always be concerned when a few people in power have written rules that govern the actions of the many who have no knowledge of those rules or how they might be applied. We should be even more concerned when people are manipulated into being bound by those rules. There have, for example, been cases where victims report their abuse only to discover that the system in which their abuse was experienced or reported has cut them off from their constitutional right to submit a suit for a trial by jury. When they signed a contract to join the church, enter into employment, or agree to mediation, they had also agreed to settle any and all legal disputes through mediation and, if necessary, binding arbitration.

Sadly, we see these external attacks launched even against helping professions like social workers, law enforcement, and health-care workers, especially within faith organizations. There have been multiple cases of faith communities teaching their members not to rely on doctors for help, that dependency upon modern medicine and procedures is a threat to one's faith. Victims in these communities have allowed children to die instead of taking them to a hospital for care when a potentially lifesaving intervention was within reach.

Sources of Understanding

You've heard the saying "knowledge is power." If education, like becoming more aware of hidden tactics of abuse, empowers you, then one of the abuser's strategies will be to dismantle your connection to those knowledge sources. For example, abuse that occurs within a religious community may involve attacks on your relationship to a higher power. Victims who view themselves as part of a much larger world that extends beyond the earthly and into the supernatural might find that supernatural realm being manipulated by the abuser as well. The abuser primarily does this by attacking the victim's understanding of good and evil. We see this even in the Bible when Satan attacked Eve's perception of God in the Garden of Eden: "Did God really say . . . ?" Similarly, an abuser might try to convince you that beliefs that might deter you from acting according to their wishes are unfounded. Many abusers have coerced the innocent into abusive situations by convincing them that there is nothing wrong with the abuse.

A thirty-year-old perpetrator preys upon a fifteen-year-old girl. He's been serving as a volunteer youth mentor in the church she's been attending. He pays her special attention and from time to time compliments her appearance. The charm increases over time as the perpetrator tests boundaries. At some point it turns into a "dating relationship," and he even promises to marry her when she turns eighteen. She knows it's not right, but he keeps telling her that God doesn't have rules that would prevent them from doing this and that God wants them to be happy. The abuser is defining for the victim what "God wants."

This is especially powerful when abusers cast themselves as agents of God. As mentioned in chapter 1, abusers can appeal to their sacred roles—their position, anointing, theological insights, or spiritual gifts—to be seen as people who know what God wants. They might even claim to have heard directly from God.

Consequently, if you find yourself in a situation like this, you may become anxious that saying no to the abuser might be the same as saying no to God himself. The abuser may offer a solution to alleviate those fears, but only in exchange for something you have that they want: your money, your endorsement, your obedience, or your body.

We see this same phenomenon at work in totalitarian regimes where the government is the sole source of information. They achieve control by making sure the people do not have access to perspectives or information that would spoil their view of the government. Or, as we've seen in the United States, a politician might claim reputable news agencies are "fake news" whenever they report information that damages the politician's image. A family can also be a small kingdom ruled by a tyrant, in which children are never afforded opportunities to hear perspectives or views that aren't approved by the controlling parent.

Putting Your World Back Together

You may feel hopeless as you consider the many ways in which another person can dismantle your life. Perhaps even now you are identifying when and where you have experienced some of these tactics and recognizing how harmful they've been in your life. Receiving a bad diagnosis is never pleasant. It is hard to look at ugly truths. It's easier to look away or numb the pain. But an important step toward healing and freedom is to look at an abusive situation under the light of truth.

It helps to consider another important truth: You do not deserve to be dismantled. You deserve to be loved. Our lives are already limited as they are. Pain and grief are often the results of experiencing these limitations—failure, sickness, addiction, death, and the like. Despite those human limitations, there is much we can become and experience as we live our one and only life. I like to think of love as helping the people around me live life to the fullest, celebrating all the ways in which they become fully alive. An abuser does the opposite. An abuser imposes limitations upon already-limited people in an already-limited world. If love is helping another person live their life to the fullest, even taking on additional limitations (like giving up a career opportunity to stay close to aging parents in need of care), then the opposite of love is putting limitations on those around you so you don't have to experience limitations yourself. The person who lacks love is the person who is either too lazy or too malicious to help others overcome their limitations. The person who hates and abuses imprisons others for their own benefit.

When you know what love is and what abuse is, then you can be better equipped to know which relationships to move away from, if it's in your power to do so, and which relationships to move toward. I hope the knowledge of these hidden tactics will not only help you avoid abusive environments but also help you find loving environments in which you can grow and thrive.

CHAPTER 4 SUMMARY

DISMANTLING YOUR EXTERNAL WORLD

Abusers groom others for abuse through dismantling their internal and external worlds. Dismantling your external world involves destroying connections between you and lifelines outside yourself: supportive relationships, institutions, and sources of understanding.

RELATIONSHIPS

By dismantling your connection to supportive relationships, abusers seek to isolate you from the people who are most likely to see through their deceptions.

INSTITUTIONS

Abusers may also seek to isolate you from institutions that provide supportive services, like journalists or members of the judicial system, that may expose or punish their abuse.

SOURCES OF UNDERSTANDING

Abusers will try to dismantle your connection to sources of information and understanding—like faith systems, news reports, or other means of education—by twisting beliefs and limiting the flow of potentially disruptive information.

CHAPTER 5

THE SILENT STRUGGLE

Once you are charmed, dismantled, and alone, the abuser advances. A thick fog descends between the charm that deceived you and the fear and shame you suddenly feel after an abusive attack. You feel paralyzed—confused and captive—caught in a web spun by the abuser under cover of darkness. Confusion produces thoughts like *I don't know what's true anymore. Maybe I am the problem? How did I get here?* Abuse impairs your ability to make sense of what is happening. It spins you around and disorients you.

Captivity produces thoughts like *I don't know what to do. I'm stuck. I encounter a wall at every turn. Worse, I fear what is behind any door I might open.* This disillusionment combined with imprisonment is a paralyzing experience.

And maybe worst of all, you feel alone.

Alone, because your world has been dismantled and you've been isolated from anyone who could support and help you. Alone, because the one person you thought you had left has betrayed you violently and blatantly. Alone, because the trauma of what you've experienced is so dark, you can't see a way out.

For many reasons, and quite understandably, it is extremely difficult for victims of abuse to speak up and expose what has happened to them. Telling their story is hard, in part, because it asks them to revisit their trauma and because they do not know how others are going to respond to their story. And there are a number of other factors that may keep them from bringing attention to their situation:

- *The belief that their credibility will be called into question.* If their story threatens the identity, power, or position of a well-known and loved individual, then people might immediately seek to discredit the story to protect the more powerful individual.
- *The belief that they have a moral responsibility to remain loyal or submissive.* Abusive communities sometimes ingrain such characteristics into followers, conditioning them to believe that to remain silent is to be a good follower.
- *A close bond with the abuser.* If the abuser is a family member, boss, friend, or coworker, victims may have a natural concern for the abuser's well-being.

- *The loss of their own reputation.* Especially if the abuser is powerful, the abuser can easily use that power to spread a narrative in which the victim is made to appear vindictive, selfish, confused, mentally ill, bitter, or in need of attention.
- *The fear of bringing public shame upon their community.* This applies in religious contexts but also in situations where exposing a member of a close-knit group would be seen as lacking in compassion, forgiveness, or love for "the family."
- *The fear of being blamed for the abuse.* Tragically, many victims have been made to believe their abuse was self-inflicted or deserved, either through their attire, attractiveness, assertive personality, or by simply being in the wrong place at the wrong time.
- *The uncertainty and unpredictability of the response.* The silence of others—even if the silence is from a lack of emotional maturity—can be unspeakably painful. Friends and family may abandon victims over what they perceive as a betrayal, especially if they are hearing other narratives spread by the accused.
- *The fear that they will be accused for not coming forward sooner. This is especially a factor if the abuse took place long in the past.* When people ask, "Why did it take so long for this to be told?" they are suggesting the survivor is at fault for not reporting the abuse sooner.

- *The threat of lawsuits after they go public with their story.*
  Some have even been told they will be "destroyed" if
  they blow the whistle. For good reasons, then, survivors
  fear losing their jobs, facing legal expenses, and ruining
  future job opportunities.
- *Potential condemnation for not following procedures
  designed to keep matters internal.* People ask, "Why
  did they have to go public?" Few, in my experience,
  understand that many victims who decide to go
  public only do so after all other appeals have
  failed.

Any one of these factors can cause a great deal of anxiety,
fear, and additional trauma. Now, it's important to note
that I'm *not* suggesting that confronting abuse is a mark
or test of courage. Choosing to never tell does not make a
victim less courageous. Usually, there are multiple motivations that exist for never telling, which can produce even
more despair. Survivors begin believing that telling others
will never accomplish anything because the barriers are
too many and too great. And so, understandably, they stay
silent and alone.

Keeping you from telling your story is one of an abuser's
goals, and they will primarily use intimidation and plea tactics to encourage your silence.

Like most human behavior,
intimidation exists
on a spectrum and can
take various forms—
it does not need to rely on
weapons or physical force.

Intimidation to Keep Silent

In addition to the silencing barriers above, the abuser plays a major role in keeping you from exposing your experience. Through intimidation, the abuser misuses their physical, verbal, spiritual, or emotional power in order to create a deep sense of danger. If the goal of charm is to draw you in, the goal of intimidation is to silence you. The wolf, no longer disguised as a friend, openly acts like a wolf.

Like most human behavior, intimidation exists on a spectrum and can take various forms—it does not need to rely on weapons or physical force. I once pushed for an investigation into the unethical behavior of my boss. When I told him I was filing formal grievances, he threatened, "I've been doing this for thirty years. You don't want to go down that road." This threat, even without any specific detail, still felt so intimidating to me. I felt that if I didn't comply, some kind of harm would come upon me and my family. Abusers can also attempt to intimidate you using . . .

- implied messages (symbolic gestures, objects, or illustrations that depict harm metaphorically—like pastor James MacDonald reportedly stabbing a butter knife into the picture of a former pastor while with fellow church leaders[1]),
- threats of lawsuits, or

- spiritual attacks (there are numerous cases of abusive spiritual leaders using the threat of a demonic attack to coerce and silence their victims).

The goal of these intimidation tactics is for you to see the abuser as powerful and to be frightened into silence. Even if nothing is said or done, simply finding yourself unexpectedly alone in the presence of a more powerful individual can create fear. Being stared down or cornered in a hallway—the slightest aggressive body language can be domineering and effective. For example, in one story I found, a youth pastor gave a girl in his student ministry a ride home from church. Instead of going the usual route, he took a back road, and before she suspected anything, he was pulling into a wooded area and parking the car in a secluded spot. In this isolated space, separate from those who might see and respond if she was in need of rescue, she rightfully feared what might be happening.

As with all the other tactics we've discussed in previous chapters, intimidation is about control, and abusers use this tactic because they already have a measure of control over their environment. Accountability is absent. This can be true even of entire boards, organizations, or communities. The less accountable an abuser is to higher authorities, the more brazen an abuser can be. Unfortunately, this often results in the organization becoming abusive as well, mirroring the abuser in their use of attacks. One of the most difficult moments for a survivor is when their story, told to the leaders of the organization with the expectation that it will be met with light—a listening ear and a compassionate heart—is instead met with darkness—a refusal to listen and a hard, cold heart—and the survivor is sent away still shaking under the weight of an unshakable yoke, still seeking escape from inescapable walls, still in possession of secrets that possess them.

Turning the Tables: Pleas as a Means of Silencing

I had just turned in my resignation after two long and painful years. I was willing to stay to assist with a smooth transition—desiring to stay, even, for the sake of saying healthy and meaningful goodbyes. The pastor, not wanting me to resign, insisted we meet one-on-one. I had grown to distrust one-on-one meetings by this point but felt I could manage it if I established some boundaries up front. Upon entering and taking the seat opposite his desk, I said, "I'm only here to discuss the details of my transition. If you want to talk about the events of the last two years, then I'm going to ask that witnesses be present."

"When did this root of bitterness begin growing in you?" he asked. "When did your anger toward me begin? And why haven't you followed Matthew 18?"

I got up to leave. As I reached for the door, the pastor began to plead, "Stay. Please stay. Wade, please. Please. Please."

I didn't know what to make of it. A condemnation

transformed into an invitation the moment I exercised my will to walk out.

An abuser can be disguised as a roaring lion one moment and take the form of a helpless lamb the next. Abusers are often not actually either lions or lambs. They are simply using disguises to deceive others into acting a certain way. The impression management literature calls this particular lamb-like tactic *supplication,* or more colloquially, pleading—any request for help, sympathy, allowance, or mercy on the basis of the person's perceived helplessness, impairment, or need. When used deceptively by an abuser, a plea can exploit our sincere desire to help and extend compassion. It is not that these extensions of mercy are not right—sometimes they are. It is that the abuser uses our compassion for their own benefit.

Whereas charms and intimidation are often used by those with greater power to control those with less power, you are more likely to encounter pleas when those with less power are trying to control those with greater power. In the meeting with my pastor, the plea came when I was ready to walk out—in that moment, I had control of the situation. Abusers perceive power in others and respond accordingly.

There are several forms that pleas can take. All are designed to keep you under the abuser's control.

The Plea of Compassion

Imagine this scenario: a lion chases a lamb into a thicket along a common road. The lamb is trapped, confused, and

When used deceptively
by an abuser,
a plea can exploit our
sincere desire to help
and extend compassion.

fearful. The lion is hard at work trying to devour the lamb when he hears a small group of shepherds approaching on foot. Afraid of being seen, he disguises himself as a lamb and jumps into the bushes on the other side of the road. To keep the shepherds from noticing and rescuing the real lamb in trouble, the lion bleats like a lamb to draw their attention. Being familiar with that cry, and thinking an innocent lamb is in need of rescue, the deceived shepherds attend to the lion, ignoring the lamb who is in real danger.

If you've been in an abusive situation, it's likely you can see yourself in that illustration. You, as the victim, suffer in silence, hoping someone might notice that something is wrong, that you've been trapped by your abuser. Yet as soon as others come close to discovering the truth, the abuser pleads for help. "I'm overwhelmed by the work. Do you realize how these people treat me despite all I do for them? I didn't sign up for this. Nobody prepared me for this situation. How would you like to be in my shoes? None of us are safe from these false accusations." Distracted, those who might otherwise help you turn away ignore the reality of the situation and focus instead on rescuing the abuser from difficulty. This tactic can be extremely hurtful to the victim.

The Plea of Obligation

Abusers will also use guilt trips as pleas, especially if they have charmed their victims through flattery and favors. When abusers need help from those they've charmed, they might seek to make a withdrawal from the bank holding all of the deposited favors.

- "After all I did for you, this is how you treat me?"
- "You owe me."
- "I was there for you when no one else was."
- "How can you betray me like this?"
- "I should never have been so kind to you."
- "Do you realize where you'd be without me?"

These statements put the burden of action and responsibility on you and leverage guilt to coerce you into actions that help the abuser.

This dynamic is seen in the well-known ploy called the "silent treatment." Like intimidation, pleas do not need to be verbalized to be communicated. The manipulator makes a deliberate choice to remain silent as a way of amplifying their appearance of hurt. You are then coerced into believing you caused them to withdraw. Because you feel guilty, even though you might have done nothing wrong, you go to the silent manipulator in an effort to end the treatment. The manipulator might then require you to meet certain conditions in order for the silence to end. By withdrawing, sulking, and withholding dialogue, the abuser can sometimes trap you in a sphere of guilt and obligation.

Perhaps one of the reasons these pleas of obligation are so effective in abusive relationships is because codependency has been slowly established. The abuser needs to maintain control over the victim, and the victim might feel the need to remain in the abuser's good favor in order to keep receiving what the abuser promises to provide, especially if the abuser is a caregiver, close friend, family member, or boss. The plea threatens to cut you off and make you out to be the one at fault. We might succumb to the plea to avoid both the loss of the relationship and the accompanying guilt.

The Plea of the Human Shield

Frank was a university president who came under fire for covering up the rape of a college student. A lawsuit brought the entire situation into the public's view, and the condemnation was swift. He initially denied the allegations. However, that one story opened the floodgates to a reservoir of hidden abuses of power. The board of trustees at the university were inundated with story after story and soon had no choice but to release their longtime president.

Frank didn't go quietly. He released a statement claiming his character was being assassinated and he didn't deserve such treatment from the board after so many years of service. He then went on to describe in detail the ways in which his wife, children, and grandchildren were supposedly affected by his exposure. "My wife and I have had to go into hiding because of all the nasty calls and letters we've received. My children fear they will face retaliation and will have a hard time keeping their careers. What do I tell my grandchildren who are reading about these horrible accusations?" Some of his supporters publicly voiced their sympathy for Frank and anger over what he was suffering. They had gotten the message and responded accordingly.

Abusers also elicit your sympathy and restraint when they use their family or others you might not want to see harmed as a shield. It's easy to imagine why this is so effective: *Should we not be concerned about their family and the effects the exposure will have on them?* If abusers believe their families can be used to quiet victims, disarm critics, and quell an outcry, then they will not hesitate to highlight, exaggerate, or fabricate the wounds being inflicted upon those closest to them. These family and friends create a human shield around the abuser. Of course, we should always speak and act with care and concern for everyone involved—and that includes an abuser's close relations—but the truth is, abusers should bear the responsibility for the damage brought about by the exposure of their actions.

The human shield does not always consist of family and friends. The abuser can use anyone who might be viewed as innocent or respectable to form this defense. In church scandals, abusive leaders can spotlight the difficulties experienced by elders and staff. People are told the exposure has made life difficult for those in leadership who had no direct involvement in the abuse but are nonetheless caught up in a crisis that they must now manage. Abusive leaders who resign might suggest they are doing so to avoid becoming a distraction and burden for the other leaders. They hide behind others' experiences, knowing people will be more inclined to avoid a confrontation with leaders they still admire and respect. People want to protect the reputation of their friends in these positions and might not pursue truth as a means of guarding seemingly innocent leaders. However, the passivity that allows abusers to renegotiate boundaries is the same passivity that prevents complicit leaders from taking ownership of their own failures and accepting the consequences of their (in)actions.

Not only does this kind of plea induce guilt in critics to silence them, but it also garners sympathy and compassion from supporters who might want to defend those they feel are being wrongly accused or mistreated.

The Plea of Injustice

I once found myself in a lunch meeting with a man who had just been released from prison for various abuses. We did not know this at the start of the lunch. He didn't disclose his imprisonment. Instead, he said he had spent some time on "sabbatical" hiding out. After we asked him a few questions about his past, he revealed the accusations and then started yelling, "I'm Brett Kavanaugh! I'm Brett Kavanaugh!" He was suggesting that the accusations against him were false by aligning his case with another case of someone being publicly maligned for what he deemed to be equally false accusations.

Abusers often plead for help by comparing themselves and their situation to infamous acts of injustice. The accused who cries, "Witch hunt!" invokes images of innocent people being pursued and burned at the stake over false beliefs, shaping people's perception of both the accused and the accusers. An exclamation of "This is a lynching!" calls to mind the brutality of a mob in carrying out unlawful executions. Let's be clear: people being burned at stakes for being witches and African Americans being lynched are entirely different scenarios from a leader being accused of abusing power. The false comparison (with its emotionally charged language) then fosters further lies about the accused and the accusers, spreading a sharp and ever-widening division: those viewed as witch hunters versus those viewed as defenders of the innocent. Sadly, these lies can even be used to justify hatred toward those who are a threat to the "innocent"—hatred that can give birth to violence.

A Final Plea: The Threat of Self-Harm

A common method abusers might use to gain sympathy and help is to threaten to harm themselves. The abuser threatens you with self-harm, exploiting your concern for their well-being. Since abuse is frequently perpetrated by those in positions of trust—those with whom you are in relationship—this particular tactic is difficult to resist.

This plea is often painfully used in the moments immediately following an assault. The abuser solicits a promise of secrecy by appealing to the ways in which they will suffer if anyone discovers their dark secret. The abuser asks *you* to

Many abusers coerce victims into silence with threats meant to give the victim the impression that telling anyone will cause some kind of destruction.

protect them, and you now bear the burden of responsibility. "This will ruin me if you ever tell anyone," they warn. You might not know what to do with such powerful secrets. Now you are told you only have one option: not to do anything. Whether explicitly stated or implied, the abuser pleads with the victim to become a co-keeper of at least two weighty secrets: (1) the truth about the abuse and (2) the truth about the abuser.

The disruptive power of these dark secrets oppresses the victim. Like any weight, the secrets become harder to carry over time. The victim feels trapped as the desire to be free from the burden of secrecy is repeatedly met with a fear of what will happen if the truth is revealed. It is a reasonable fear. Many abusers coerce victims into silence with threats meant to give the victim the impression that telling anyone will cause some kind of destruction.

The most powerful plea of this type is undoubtedly to be rescued from a threat of suicide. Whether or not the threat of suicide is legitimate, hearing from another person that they might take their own life will cause any caring person to respond with concern. Nothing is quite so infuriating as an abuser who wounds someone deeply and then attempts to keep the wounded person under their control by threatening suicide if the abuse is ever made public.

Imagine a high-profile person in a position of power, reputation, and wealth who has been sexually abusing another adult in their life. The abuse has been kept hidden from family, friends, and colleagues. Eventually, the adult victim decides to escape from the abusive situation. The abuser fears what will happen to him if the victim decides to tell someone. He'll likely lose his position, reputation, and wealth. He cannot bear to know that his secret could be out. So he messages her repeatedly, pleading with her to not walk away. When she refuses, he mentions his depressed state and how he doesn't think he could live without her, that he might as well just end it all. What is she to do? She might feel the weight of the plea and do whatever she must to prevent him from carrying out the threat.

The plea of self-harm can be a powerful tool for an abuser to regain power over you. Part of its power is due to the fact that it can be difficult to know how to respond. It is our natural desire to extend compassion to those who express their pain to us. It can seem very difficult, impossible even, to respond in a way that protects ourselves while not risking the harm the abuser threatens will come to them. However, in our effort to be gracious, we can sometimes lose sight of what is true. Compassion without truth can be a product of deception. If it's safe to do so, I have found it helpful to say something like, "I am concerned for you, and I want to be compassionate, but I also want to acknowledge what is true. Here's what I know to be true . . ." As part of that, you might even speak the truth about how the other person is using guilt, fear, and obligation to manipulate you. Taking an inventory of what is true could also lead you to a realization of your own need for safety, boundaries, and changes. And if the other person is an abuser, then an inventory of truth will affirm that reality and remind you that the responsibility for any suffering they experience as a result of their own behavior is theirs and theirs alone. You can hold space for what is true about the abuse, for what you must do to protect yourself, and for the sorrow you feel over the difficult situation the abuser has caused.

Reclaiming Your Voice

Choosing to expose an abuser, especially one with power, carries great risk. There are many strong motivations for a victim to never tell their story, as we saw in this chapter. Therefore, when a victim does speak out, it is usually because they are in desperate need of help or are concerned that others might be in harm's way and are compelled to act despite the risks.

If you are at a point of wanting freedom from the confusion and captivity but fear the consequences of taking the necessary steps, know that you are not alone and that your feelings are normal. I can't tell you what to do—every situation is complex and particular—and there isn't a road map I can give you. But every act you take to resist the charm, stop the dismantling, and reclaim your voice is an act that will bring you closer to truth and freedom.

And there are small steps you can take. Let's say you believe your work environment is unhealthy but you aren't sure if you are assessing the problem accurately. Simply talking to someone in another work environment might give you the perspective you need and will help you practice using your voice.

Meeting with a competent, trauma-informed therapist can bring clarity to confusion, as the therapist helps disentangle the webs the abuser has weaved. Any space that affords you the opportunity to tell your story in an unrushed manner will be helpful to you. You may not be able to tell it all at once, or in a way that you think will make sense to the other person, but a trauma-informed supporter will honor where you are.

If telling a professional is not an option yet, then consider calling a hotline or writing in an online chat, like the National Sexual Assault Telephone Hotline facilitated by RAINN (Rape, Abuse & Incest National Network).

If telling another is not something you are ready for, then, as I recommended earlier, consider telling yourself. Write down what you would tell someone if you had the opportunity. Writing your experience out on paper can be a courageous act of resistance and survival.

Surviving is not simple or easy. There are many threads to disentangle, many ruins that need to be rebuilt, many words that need to be found. If you can't shout, find a way to whisper. If you can't rebuild the ruins all at once, find a small place to start. Again, if all you can say is "Something's not right," then begin there. It might be just the word of truth needed to stop the web of lies from growing.

CHAPTER 5 SUMMARY

THE SILENT STRUGGLE

There are many reasons why someone might keep silent in the face of abuse. There are personal reasons (like the way speaking up might be viewed) in addition to tactics an abuser might employ—tactics like intimidation and pleas.

PERSONAL REASONS

A combination of fear and unpredictability may lead a person to stay silent about abuse—fear of retaliation from the abuser and their followers or unpredictability about how others will respond to the abuse.

INTIMIDATION

Abusers may use intimidation—which can be threats of violence, lawsuits, or spiritual attacks, or which may be symbolic messages of implied harm—to coerce you into silence.

PLEAS

Abusers who fear they may be exposed may use plea tactics to secure your silence. Pleas can take several forms, appealing to your compassion, obligations, or sense of justice, or warning that exposure may cause harm to themselves or innocent others.

CHAPTER 6

ON
THE
DEFENSE

Barry had long feared that the young woman he had assaulted might one day speak out. He had often thought about what he might say if people ever discovered what he had done. The abuse wasn't the only secret he was hiding. He knew how to play the part of a young professional. He was well liked, smart, and could easily hold down a job. But his personal life was in shambles. He was losing self-control in many areas of life, and addictions were haunting him. His life was splitting apart, and the only way he could hold it together was by learning to lie. So when ten years later people found out he had assaulted a woman, he was, in some ways, ready to defend himself with a fortress of learned deception.

Barry's story is not unique. The Old Testament prophet Micah described a person who invents lies as a "man of wind."[1] The deceptive person wraps you in a wind of words. Words are tossed around you, making them difficult to grasp and hold on to. You struggle to find your way as the wind pushes against you. And when the man of wind leaves, those who have been destroyed by the lies are left to pick up the debris and begin rebuilding.

The winds of deception are fiercest and most destructive when truth is close at hand. It is at this point that the deceiver goes on the defensive, and the tactics used to evade exposure are usually greater in number and complexity than the tactics used to groom others for abuse.

On the offensive, the abuser can take time to charm, dismantle, and plead because they have the luxury of planning, scheming, and making calculations. Their traps are laid, and all they have to do is wait. But when they're exposed, the abuser no longer has the luxury to wait, and they will abandon these tactics. Suddenly, the abuser isn't in control—a position that is extremely unsettling to them. To be on the defensive, then, they must learn to react quickly and with increasing intuition at every turn as their web of lies is untangled.

My extensive research into crisis events reveals four types of defenses abusers are likely to use when confronted: *denials, excuses, justifications,* and *comparisons.* Sometimes these are used interchangeably, but most often they are used one after the other, a blueprint of predictable behavior. Imagine a

Abusers are likely to use four types of defenses when confronted: *denials, excuses, justifications,* and *comparisons.*

fortress protected by several walls. The outer wall, the wall that serves as the first defense, is typically the wall of denial. If the wall of denial fails to repel the truth, truth seekers will encounter the wall of excuse. If they find their way through, over, or past that wall, they'll be met by the wall of justification. And if that wall fails to stop them, then they can expect to face the wall of comparisons.

Each wall is made of different material, but each functions to prevent the discovery of truth. While these walls are built with speed and power, complicating matters for you as a truth seeker, they are not insurmountable. If you know what each barrier is made of, you can learn how to get past them and fight for justice.

The Wall of Denial

We have all heard the classic version of denial: an angry, red-faced "That is not true!" Many criminals have begun their failed defense efforts with an outright denial, only to later confess or be convicted on the basis of evidence. But not every denial is so black and white. Often, if you raise an accusation or question about an abuser's behavior, the first line of defense is a denial that leads people to doubt the merits of the accusation—or you as the victim. If the abuser can convince the community that their behavior is being fabricated, exaggerated, or otherwise misrepresented, they can divert attention away from themselves. So when the abuser says, "That is categorically false; I would never do such a thing,"

Walls of Defense

DENIAL

The abuser subtly or overtly casts doubt on an accusation

EXCUSES

The abuser acknowledges something wrong has been done, but casts blame on another party

JUSTIFICATIONS

The abuser rationalizes the wrongdoing

COMPARISONS

The abuser uses other issues or people as examples to make the wrongdoing seem less serious

the community turns their attention to asking questions like "Why would a victim lie about this? Is this about attention? Is it a money-grab?" Suddenly the focus of investigation is on the accuser and not the accused.

A denial can also appear in overt ways. A young woman attended a monthly elders' meeting at her church to participate in a discussion on the church's ministry to children. Numerous church members had been raising concerns over the leadership's decision to cut some children's programming. She asked them, "In what ways is the church investing in children?" Clearly perturbed by the question, one elder responded, "Do you think I'd allow my daughter to participate in the children's programming if I didn't think we were investing in children?" His implicit denial of the behavior was presented by reframing the question, putting the woman on the defensive. Not surprisingly, the young woman dropped the question and shortly afterward left the meeting. Responses like the ones this young woman received teach followers not to question the decisions of their leaders. The walls surrounding the powerful become like a prison that the community knows exists but do not dare approach or discuss.

The Wall of Excuses

After denial, an abuser will likely move to the next line of defense: making excuses. An excuse acknowledges that a wrong has occurred but shifts responsibility or blame for the wrong from the shoulders of the person making the excuse. An excuse concedes the basic facts of a wrong that a denial will not. However, an excuse will stop short of accepting personal responsibility for the harm caused. Whether an excuse is legitimate is an important ethical and moral question. Let's explore three common types of excuses.

The Excuse of Intent

More often than not, we are unable to discern a person's motive with certainty, and because of that, abusers are likely to use this line of defense. This type of excuse, for example, is a classic tactic of the sexual predator who engages in tickling, wrestling, and other forms of unwanted touch. The scenario the predator creates here can be quickly excused as accidental, even if it's completely intentional. In other situations of abuse, the abuser might attempt to excuse themselves by denying the behavior was motivated by evil:

- "It was a youthful indiscretion."
- "A dark moment came over me."
- "I made a mistake."
- "I never meant to make you feel uncomfortable or do anything you didn't want to do."
- "I stumbled into sin."

Each of these statements frames the abuse as accidental in some way, knowing that people are quick to excuse someone who unknowingly or without malice causes harm. The deceived community, when they accept these excuses, then mirrors them. "Oh, we've all made mistakes," they might say. "Who are we to judge?"

I pray that communities dealing with an exposed abuser learn to pause before accepting excuses simply because they do not want to be bothered or because they do not want to consider that the accused might be capable of intentional wrongdoing. True, it's not necessary to jump to conclusions about the intention or character of someone who has been accused. But even if it's not wise to ascribe motive, communities must address behavior—and what that behavior communicates. If they don't, they risk sending a message to other would-be offenders that they are susceptible to deceptive and

Insufficient training or lack of foresight is not an acceptable excuse for leaders charged with the duty to protect the organization's members.

destructive individuals. The abolitionist Elizabeth Heyrick argued this point when she wrote, "Unsuccessful opposition to crimes of every description invariably increases their power and malignity."[2]

The Excuse of Ability

Similar to the excuse of intent, an abuser may use the excuse of ability to distract their accusers. That is, they argue that they did not have the power to make a different decision. They were impaired in some way—drunk, stressed, exhausted, on different medication—and if it weren't for that impairment, they would have acted responsibly. In one case I came across in my research, a man claimed to have had no knowledge that he had violently killed his wife during his sleep until he woke up the next morning.

A common excuse of ability that organizations use is the suggestion that those in positions to respond were not prepared through education and training. "If we knew then what we know now, of course we would have responded with care and competence." Typically, the reason they are receiving such information to begin with is that others view them as able to respond intelligently, or at least to have the wisdom to defer decision making to those who can. Once an organization assumes the responsibility that comes with being in charge, they assume the obligation to make sure they are adequately equipped to exercise their authority. Insufficient training or lack of foresight is not an acceptable excuse for leaders charged with the duty to protect the organization's members.

Abusers also deny ability when they claim they did not possess the authority to make a certain decision or take a different course of action. This is similar to the person who says, "I need to stay in my lane" or "It's not my place" or "It's none of my business." Again, sometimes there is a need to recognize the limitations of authority. However, it is always necessary to ask, "Is this a legitimate excuse for this situation?"

Sometimes there are higher values we must adhere to than the value of respecting authority, especially if that authority is asking us to be complicit with evil. The parable of the Good Samaritan, told by Jesus in Luke 10, exposes fault with the excuse that says, "It isn't my responsibility." As a Christian, my ethic demands I consider all possible ways to overcome obstacles instead of using those obstacles as an excuse. Victims suffer and are left to perish when those in positions to help suggest they lack the ability. It is extremely painful—not to mention rejecting and devaluing—to witness others step by and over you while you are suffering. The road from Jerusalem to Jericho, a perilous route, provided the setting for Jesus' parable of the Good Samaritan, and travelers were susceptible to ambush. Martin Luther King Jr. suggested that maybe the priest and the Levite were thinking to themselves, *What will happen to me if I cross the road to help?* instead of asking, *What will happen to the wounded if I don't cross the road to help?*[3] Those who desire to follow Jesus must take the risk to show love instead of hiding behind excuses—and accepting excuses of ability from our leaders.

The Excuse of Agency

A third type of excuse shifts agency. This is classic blaming. It says, "I am not the primary agent of harm." The person in the wrong points their finger at someone else. Excuses of agency go all the way back to the Garden of Eden, when God asked Adam, "Did you eat from the tree that I commanded you not to eat from?" Adam replied, "The woman You gave to be with me—she gave me some fruit from the tree, and I ate." So God asked Eve, "What is this you have done?" And Eve further passed the blame: "It was the serpent. He deceived me, and I ate."[4] Both Adam and Eve pointed the finger at someone else as the reason for their wrongdoing. What would have happened—how might our world be different—if instead they had accepted responsibility for their actions?

It is normal to want to shake off shame. That's what excuses do. They say, "Even though something bad has happened, *I* acted in a legitimate manner." Threatened legitimacy—the idea that we have the right to act, think, or decide in a certain way because of who we are or the role we occupy—threatens a person's identity, and a threatened identity fosters shame. No one wants to bear shame, nor should we rejoice when we see shame weighing down another. The answer is for the person at fault to acknowledge the truth of the shame, to face it and say without excuse, "I am ashamed of my behavior." Only then can they forgive, make restitution, and heal the wounds they've caused.

The Wall of Justifications

Once the offense is clearly exposed and the question of who is at fault is undeniably answered, the abuser or abusive organization may begin to justify the behavior. The tactics of justification and excuses are very similar and serve a similar purpose; however, the difference is that while excuses shape your perception of the *wrongdoer*, justifications shape your perception of the *wrong*.

Imagine you are sitting in your parked car along a busy street waiting for a friend when another car hits your rear bumper while attempting to pull into the space behind you. You and the other driver get out to inspect the damage. The driver who hit your car could offer a variety of excuses: "I didn't see your car parked there" or "My foot slipped off the brake" or "My kids were distracting me." Each of these seeks to escape or lessen the driver's responsibility by focusing on something influencing them. Or the driver could focus on the state of your car in an effort to find justification. They might suggest that you had not pulled fully into your parking spot or that, after all, no damage was done. This is justification.

We *excuse* actors and *justify* actions. In cases of abuse, justifications hinge on an invented scale that the abuser uses to give the impression that you are not a "true" victim. They draw attention to factors such as your background, attire, personality, past relationships, or motives to push you down on the "victim scale" so you are more likely than them to receive the blame. Sometimes they may even target your past, seeking something that would suggest *you* are the one with the pattern of bad behavior and that you corrupted the abuser. Every time a victim is called a "Jezebel" or people comment, "She knew what she was doing" or "She's not innocent either," the spotlight is wrongly put on the victim, and the scales are tipped toward the abuser. Similarly, abusers may draw attention to circumstances around the abuse that suggest it wasn't really a big deal.

The Wall of Comparisons

The final wall of defense for an abuser or abusive organization is comparison. By drawing comparisons between themselves and issues or people indirectly related to the central truths of the abuse, they try to show why their wrongs shouldn't be held against them. They accept responsibility and acknowledge the harm but try to establish comparisons—like precedents and examples—for why it wouldn't be fair to impose consequences on themselves. Here are several of the most common comparisons abusers might make.

Comparisons to Greater Wrongs

"There are real problems in the world you should be concerned about instead of wasting your time worrying about me." Ron was upset that his outbursts were finally being confronted. He had learned to get his way by intimidating his employees whenever they questioned his authority or failed to meet a deadline. He thought the fastest way to get people to fall in line was to raise his voice and threaten to fire them. The board held a meeting to confront him after they received numerous letters from employees. He couldn't deny his outbursts, and he knew the negative impact it was having on the team, but he figured he might convince the board that they were allowing themselves to turn a molehill into a mountain.

Comparison can seem like a strong wall to hide behind. A deceptive offender might catalog more serious examples of wrongs, then boast how they are not like those who committed such acts. *They've* never engaged in such horrible behavior, and they would even go out of their way to oppose such behavior. By minimizing their own actions in comparison to more horrific wrongs, the abuser's goal is to lead you to believe that just as they are not connected to the more serious actions they describe, so they should not be connected to the less serious actions they are accused of. It's kind of like the justification that denies real injury, but since the injury itself cannot be denied, it is simply minimized when viewed in comparison to a supposed greater example of harm. Perhaps the most telling sign that harm is being minimized is when a person begins their defense with the words, "It's not like he . . ." or "He didn't actually . . ." Statements such as "It's not like he raped her or anything" or "He didn't actually assault her physically" minimize the gravity of the harm and build a case that favors the abuser.

Comparisons to Cultural Standards

Jack was a married man who was known for his crude talk and sexual jokes. Most people let him be until he decided to run for a position on the district school board. A few parents voiced their concerns and were immediately met with opposition. Some said, "He's just a man being a man." When asked about his language, Jack passed it off as "locker-room talk" and suggested that all men talk like that from time to time. Many people were willing to accept these explanations—"That's just Jack"—until a woman came forward with an allegation of sexual harassment against Jack. She was fifteen and working at a restaurant at the time she met him. Jack was a single, thirty-year-old cook. Surely the news of this behavior, coupled with the widespread knowledge of Jack's coarse language, would mark the end of his pursuit of a position on the school board. But people close to him began suggesting that Jack was from a culture where it wasn't unusual for older men to date or pursue teenage girls. "People had different standards back then," they'd claim.

In this story, Jack and his supporters drew comparisons to what they believed (or wanted others to believe) were normal behaviors within a particular culture. By comparing their behavior to cultural norms, abusers strive to maintain acceptance and escape accountability. Their behavior is simply a product of the culture they are from.

These comparisons to cultural standards can also be used to reject a need to follow laws. Society is made safer through laws and the enforcement of those laws, laws that are thankfully being updated each year as our understanding of abuse grows. Some, however, resist these changes because they force individuals and institutions to change their practices.

For example, churches have attempted to address abuse on their own without involving authorities because it is simply how they have "always handled such matters." New laws demand that they update their policies and procedures. When asked why they chose to cover up an abuse instead of reporting it in accordance with state laws, an institution might appeal to their historical practice. It's a manifestation of the claim that says, "We've always done it this way."

Like many of these types of comparisons, the lie is found in the association and in the implications of the association. Joking about sexual harassment, for example, is not typical locker-room talk, at least not in the locker rooms I've been in.

The implication is that if our culture accepts such behavior in general, then that same culture should accept the specific behavior in question, or at least provide allowance until the culture changes or the person who is a product of the culture is given the opportunity to be deculturated.

Comparisons to Industry Standards

Defenses of institutional abuses often include a comparison to normal behavior or standard expectations within a certain industry or field. For example, a university exposed for its poor and dangerous responses to abuse survivors argued that it was operating according to procedures typical of higher education at the time, at one point suggesting that all of higher education was attempting to catch up with the issues surrounding abuse.

I've witnessed more than one church compare their poor response to abuse allegations to what they believed to be an overall poor readiness level among all churches. "We are certainly ahead of most churches when it comes to our response to these issues." These appeals to standards are defensive and lack any data to make meaningful comparisons with other churches. It is the same defense made by those who appeal to greater wrongs. A church might provide another church that does not conduct background checks as a model to compare itself against and then boast about how they are not like that church.

Similarly, they might create a thread between themselves

and others whom people view favorably, like name-dropping. They draw attention to another respected individual or group and then boast about their positive connection with them. They try to get under someone else's umbrella to escape the weather when their own umbrella is no longer able to withstand the storm. I became involved in assisting an organization in the midst of crisis after the president pushed decisions through that he said went through an approval process when they actually had not. In another case I researched, an organization compared their responses to abuse with that of a well-respected psychologist, which the psychologist later took offense to. I've observed a definite pattern across cases of institutional abuse in which the abuser of power claimed that a decision or action had received approval or endorsement when it actually had not.

This is how endorsements within a field are exploited by an exposed leader. The leader might reach out to endorsers for protection when their legitimacy is threatened. The powerful friends within their field might be able to give them a platform with an audience that will hear their narrative, or they might provide them with access to a network of crisis managers, public relations professionals, lawyers, politicians, or other powerful individuals. Abusers quickly identify who their supporters are and then use flattery, compliments, bribes, and other charms to thread themselves to potential supporters. If that support is public, then the exposed abuser will publicly enhance their endorsers' positive attributes in order to bolster the credibility of their judgment. The more people favor the people the abuser is positively connected to, the more likely they are to support the abuser's arguments. These industry networks of endorsers provide abusers with a powerful base from which their narratives can be promulgated. Judith Herman wrote, "The more powerful the perpetrator, the greater is his prerogative to name and define reality, and the more completely his arguments prevail."[5]

Comparisons to Good Deeds

Abusers and their enablers might weave together the abuser's life's work in general and their contribution to that work in particular to downplay their role or mitigate the consequences for abuse. This is often seen in response to a specific question about a specific behavior. Rather than address the details of their behavior, they spotlight their life in general because it is easier to defend. This tactic subtly diverts attention away from any specific words or actions they know are more difficult to explain.

They might at this point bring attention to all the people they have helped throughout their life. They might say their accusers are launching a campaign against their "good name" and that perhaps jealousy is at work. One abuser suggested his accuser was simply upset that he kept climbing in his career while his accuser's career faltered.

Abusers may go so far as to add their family members

to this portion of the web, returning to the "human shield" tactic we looked at in the last chapter. By connecting you to the perceived negative effects the allegations are having on their family, the abuser pours more condemnation on you and requests more help from supporters. This is a common tactic in which the abuser uses someone who is innocent as a shield to deflect accusation from the abuser. They become a part of the good and innocent portions of the abuser's life that the abuser presents in hopes of escaping consequences.

They might compare their wrong to the good they've accomplished since the abuse, suggesting that they've learned their lesson and have changed. This tactic can be particularly effective, but the problem is that, when used deceptively, it fails to identify specific good deeds that were pursued to restore what was taken from the victim. No amount of good the abuser has done for *others* can remove from the need to do what is right for the person they abused.

Some might even appeal to the greater good in an effort to show that the abuse somehow produced positive traits in the victim: traits like resilience, courage, and endurance. The abuser can claim the wrongs made them more qualified to help others who engage in similar abuses. It's worth noting that in comparisons like this, either the abuser or well-meaning others might make unhelpful statements to victims that seek to show why the abuse was used for good in their life or that God meant it for their good. I believe it is important for survivors to decide for themselves how their abuse should be framed. Others should not rush to ascribe meaning to another person's trauma.

Getting Past the Walls

To be clear, there are legitimate and appropriate defenses. We all have the right to defend ourselves when wrongly accused. Our legal system functions on the premise of "innocent until proven guilty." So how do you know that a wall is simply a defense designed to hide the truth and not a legitimate denial, excuse, justification, or comparison?

Because these walls tend to be built in a layered, sequential way, the most important wall to get through is the wall of denial. To get past this thick wall often requires outside investigation into the facts of what happened. In the absence of a confession, it will be necessary to pursue an objective process of fact-finding. Hopefully, those in positions of authority will pursue an independent investigation as soon as a credible allegation is brought to their attention. If not, then the victim might decide to appeal directly to an oversight agency for accountability, if one exists, or take additional measures like speaking with other potential victims or advocates or involving investigative journalists. I always recommend that people keep appealing to the next highest authority until action is taken. Once the offender reaches a point of no longer being able to deny what happened—it's no longer just one person's word against another's—then the other walls should be easier to overcome.

Once the offender reaches a point of no longer being able to deny what happened, then the other walls should be easier to overcome.

Walls of excuse, justification, and comparison can be challenged by asking the question, "Is this a legitimate excuse, justification, or comparison?" Even if the claim itself is true, it is not always the case that the truthfulness of the claim is an adequate defense. For example, when a mandatory reporter of child abuse fails to report suspected abuse and then claims, "I didn't know what the law was," that excuse can be challenged by saying, "You had an obligation to be familiar with the laws when you accepted the duty to care for children." In this case, the excuse of ability is not legitimate.

It is always hard to poke at a person's defensive walls. The other person will then see you as a threat. You might be attacked in some way for daring to challenge the abuser's defense. They need you to accept their explanation because, by this point, they are exposed and running out of options. They feel vulnerable. A person accustomed to power might become dangerous when they begin to feel powerless. As you confront these defenses, keep in mind your need for safety. Think through a plan for protecting yourself. It is unlikely these walls of defense will crumble without a fight. Be safe. Be careful. And if possible, ask others to support you.

CHAPTER 6 SUMMARY

ON THE DEFENSE

Once an abuser is in danger of being exposed, they will put up several walls of defense to try to prevent exposure or minimize the blame they receive. Most often truth seekers will have to make it through four successive defenses to reveal the truth: walls of denial, excuse, justification, and comparison.

DENIALS

Abusers will likely first try to deny claims that any abuse has happened. An objective fact-finding investigation is often the clearest way through this wall.

EXCUSES

Once the abuse can no longer be denied, abusers will offer excuses: yes, a wrong happened, but they are not to blame. They often use excuses of intent, ability, or agency to deflect blame from themselves and cast blame somewhere else.

JUSTIFICATIONS

If others do not accept their excuses, abusers will move to justifications in an attempt to shape the way others perceive the wrong.

COMPARISONS

Finally, if the other walls do not repel the truth, abusers will try to minimize the seriousness of their wrong by comparing it with other, worse wrongs, by appealing to cultural or industry standards, or by highlighting their past good deeds.

CONCESSIONS

Exhausted. It's the word that came to mind each time Monica got an opportunity to stop and reflect. She had been fighting for truth and justice for more than two years after having been victimized by her narcissistic and abusive boss. She was not prepared for the difficulties that would confront her once she spoke out about her abuse. Now, two years since breaking her silence, the board was finally apologizing. Their statement contained many of the words you'd expect: "We are sorry . . . mistakes were made . . . we promise to improve." However, something didn't seem right about the apology. It felt impersonal, awkward, and contrived. But what would happen if she rejected the apology? The past two years certainly weren't easy—she had lost relationships and, in some circles, her reputation. She feared more rejection from those who still couldn't understand why this fight was even necessary, all these years later. Would the few who remained on her side turn their backs as well?

And more than anything, she was tired. At one point, she had faced a wall of denial, then one of excuse, then of justification, and finally of comparison. Now, having no other defense left, those in the wrong were prepared to concede. Accepting the apology would mark the end of her battle. Then she could rest. Some saw the apology as a first step and told her she was expecting too much, too soon. "The important thing is they are moving in the right direction now," they remarked. She wasn't so sure, and those doubts plagued her. *They just don't get it*, she thought.

Though the statement was labeled an apology, Monica was actually on the receiving end of what I call a concession. The reason something seemed off was that the board's apology was not being offered out of a concern for what was right (as a true apology always is), but rather as the next tactic to achieve their goal: quelling the scandal. They were willing to say, "We are sorry," as long as it would result in Monica's retreat; she was becoming too much of a threat to their secrets.

When the abuser knows they've been caught, the words "I'm sorry" are often casually offered to the weary victim in hopes they will be left alone, as if those two words were a magical key to a place where every grievance is immediately resolved and every wound automatically healed. "We did what you wanted; we apologized," the board told Monica after she informed them she couldn't accept their apology. In the end, you see, it was still about *them*: what *they* needed to move on, what defined an acceptable apology in *their* eyes, how *they* could maintain a level of power in the situation. They waved their white flag of surrender in hopes they could turn away a threat without having to bear anything beyond the shame of a simple concession.

This is really what it comes down to when abuse is exposed, when darkness is brought to light: Who will do whatever it takes to overcome a scandal, and who will do all they must to pursue what is right? Those who are governed by integrity will do whatever it takes to establish the truth and correct wrongs, even if it means giving up their power. Those governed by power will do only what is necessary to prevent or quell scandal so as to not risk losing that power. They are crisis managers, first and foremost, not truth seekers. Even the decision to apologize is a calculation made out of a concern for the self and not out of a concern for the person who has been harmed. There are no shortcuts to authentic confession, restitution, and repair. A person must know what it is they have done and the harm they have caused before they can even hope to offer an apology that heals. Truth must always precede confession, and an apology offered without a full acknowledgment of the truth is more likely a concession—a tactic designed to disarm a threat.

The Root of Shame

My experience and research have shown me that concessions, while offered as a bridge of reconciliation, are often

This is what it comes down to
when abuse is exposed:
Who will do whatever it takes
to overcome a scandal,
and who will do all they must
to pursue what is right?

surrounded by other messages that serve a very different purpose. This bridge of reconciliation is surrounded by barriers
of defense and self-promotion—and more than anything,
the bridge is used as a means of avoiding the murky waters
of shame. Abusers and abusive organizations may concede
the basic reality of the wrong—"Yes, this happened"—but
quickly add statements that either soften their responsibility
or promote their integrity: "We value all people and only
want what is best for everyone involved." If these concessions
do their job, the accused will stay in power, stay in favor with
the community, and stay far from the shame their actions
deserve.

The problem with that, of course, is that the shame then
remains squarely on the shoulders of victims. It has to go
somewhere. In the eyes of the abuser, keeping the shame on
the victim means that their side—their actions—have legitimacy. Legitimacy, again, is the state of feeling confident that
you are in the right. For abusers, they want others to see
them as legitimate, even if they themselves know they are
in the wrong. Shame, on the other hand, is the state of feeling humiliated because you believe you are in the wrong.
Abusers want to be sure others do not see them as the bearers
of shame. This battle between shame and legitimacy is often
at the heart of cover-ups. This is also why abusers find it so
difficult, if not impossible, to truly apologize. Perhaps the
shame would expose their illegitimacy, and they would lose
what is no longer their right to have: following, influence,
position, money, and power. And so they fearfully run from

public shame, like thieves being chased while clutching their stolen goods. The more they feel their treasures slipping from their fingers, the more desperate they become, and the more frantic they will be in their attempt to hold on to whatever they still can.

This battle for legitimacy is also why you may receive an "apology" but still feel as if you are the one in the wrong. Unfortunately, victims are already primed to believe the shame-based messages they receive, especially from their abusers. Out of a desire to clear the air, you might be the first to acknowledge what you perceive to be the mistakes you made, might be the first to apologize because you've been made to feel as if you are the flaw in the equation. A concession can allow you to remain plagued with shame-based thoughts like, *Maybe I am making too much of this. I shouldn't have made such a fuss. They don't deserve this. After all, I could have done more to prevent it.*

This is why some of the most important words you can hear from others are, "It's not your fault. You did nothing wrong. You have nothing to be ashamed of." It will likely take time to believe such messages are true, but it is important you hear them. An authentic apology acknowledges the correct distribution of shame.

The Anatomy of Concession

People who hear the words "I'm sorry" and observe what appears, on the surface, to be a new kind of response must remember the deceptive nature of abuse. While you should always hope for truth and advocate for change, you should expect deception and consider the possibility that these new words and actions do not reflect a genuine apology but are the predictable next steps in the direction the abuser has always been moving—a course that takes the abuser as far away from shame and as close to legitimacy as possible.

How can you tell the difference between an apology and a simple concession? An authentic apology, especially when it is offered in response to significant and long-term harm, will be so clearly distinct from every prior experience that it will be unquestionably received. It will appear like a flash of light in a darkened room, like an exploding clap of thunder in the dead of night, like the unveiling of a hidden treasure, like a resurrection from the dead—not because of any of the apologizer's qualities but because of the innate power of truth. Elizabeth Heyrick wrote, "Truth and justice, make their best way in the world, when they appear in bold and simple majesty; their demands are most willingly conceded when they are most fearlessly claimed."[1] A truth-filled apology will contain a majestic quality. A concession, on the other hand, will lack that freeing quality. It does more to confuse than heal because it doesn't name specific wrongs, so you are left feeling unsure of what the wrongdoer is taking responsibility for. A concession is frustrating because it makes you wonder if they really "get it." And it traps you because refusing to accept the "apology" will likely lead to further tension.

A concession tends to be as short as possible, nonspecific,

and packaged in defensive language. It's a throwing up of the hands, as if to say, "All right! You caught me." The individual or organization will try to con their way out of facing the consequences. They expect their pseudo-apology to be a ticket to immediate escape. "We've said we're sorry; now let's move on." Really, what they're saying is, "This remains an obstacle to our future success, so let's do what we need to step over it without being tripped up."

There are key phrases to look for in a concession: "I'm sorry for the miscommunication." "I'm sorry you feel that way." "I apologize you experienced me in that manner." "I'm sorry I made you uncomfortable." More important than these, though, you should be on the lookout for what *isn't* said. What did you expect to hear and want to hear but didn't?

Bottom line: if you have to analyze whether an apology is authentic, it probably isn't. But here are some additional things to watch out for to determine whether an apology is genuine or a concession.

The Concession That Condemns

One church was rocked when a number of women published a blog post detailing allegations against the church and its lead pastor for the abuse of multiple members over a period of many years. The blog post claimed that members of the board did not act on the allegations they had received years earlier. Now journalists were calling, and concerned members were showing up at the church offices looking for answers. The leaders scrambled to get a statement put together to send to their members. It read, in part, "We are grieved whenever people are abused. While we are aware of our need to address some deficiencies that have been brought to light and are deeply sorry for any mistakes we've made, we want to encourage people to come directly to us with their concerns. We would all be wise not to ignore the clear biblical teachings on handling disputes with one another. These instructions are meant to protect everyone involved."[2] This statement sent a clear message: "Yes, there is truth to what has been published about us, but it was wrong for that truth to be published."

Concessions can take various forms, and the concession that condemns is typically offered in anger or frustration. Perhaps the most common example is the apology that says, "I'm sorry you feel that way." If you've ever been on the receiving end of this kind of statement, you know this isn't an apology; it's a condemnation, a subtle suggestion that your feelings are not based in reality. The apologizer is unwilling to acknowledge their wrongs and instead argues that the fault lies with the person who is feeling wronged.

The person is not apologizing out of remorse for the hurt they have caused but out of frustration for what they believe is a subjective interpretation of their behavior, an interpretation they claim misrepresents them. So rather than honoring the legitimacy of the hurt, they want the other person to feel ashamed for feeling hurt. People who condemn the person they are saying "I'm sorry" to likely believe they are being misrepresented and are being forced into an apology.

The Concession That Appeases

Avery knew his outbursts of anger toward his coworkers would one day get him in trouble. He was the vice president at a large nonprofit. He felt safe throwing his weight around because he had gotten away with it for so long, and besides, the president was a longtime friend and would likely have his back if he ever needed it. That day had finally arrived. A few employees had written up a complaint and sent it to the chairman of the board and the president. They quickly called a meeting with Avery. Before they could even begin, Avery quickly inserted, "I know what this is about. I'm sorry. It won't happen again." They understood each other, and it was a quick meeting. Not too many months passed before Avery found a way to restructure his area and remove the positions of those who had complained about his behavior.

There are times when a person apologizes simply to appease the demands of someone with greater power. They apologize because they do not want to face the repercussions of not obeying an authority figure. For example, an employee might apologize simply because their boss requires it. In a similar manner, organizations might issue a statement of apology only after an outcry from constituents or pressure from external accountability structures has grown strong enough to demand it. Such apologies rarely lead to change because extrinsic motivation—motivation due to factors outside of a person or organization—does not possess the lasting and steadfast movement necessary for restorative work. Intrinsic motivation—the will fueled by internal factors like integrity and compassion—is required for an apology to be authentic.

The Concession That Excuses

If the apologizer still believes defenses are available, then they will likely attach some excuses or justifications to their apology. In the context of an apology, these defenses are sometimes preceded by the disclaimer, "This isn't an excuse, but . . ." Each time I hear this phrase tucked into an apology, it is almost always, ironically enough, followed by an excuse or justification.

Here are some of the most common excuses that accompany a pseudo-apology. I call these "apoloscuses."

1. *"It was never my intention to . . ."* This is perhaps the most common excuse and is typically driven by a desire to escape or reduce consequences because people tend to excuse innocent mistakes. Words like *mistake, blunder, fall, trip, stumble,* and *mishap* are used when the person is seeking to deny any ill intent.

2. *"Mistakes were made."* In its most basic form, and perhaps most subtle, this apoloscuse removes the apologizer from the language of the apology. "Mistakes were made" is a passive and weak substitute

for the more direct "I (or we) made mistakes." The apologizer might also shift ownership by suggesting someone else is partly to blame. Or they might highlight reasons why it would be unreasonable to hold them fully responsible. Organizations do this when they say, "This happened before the current leadership" or "The injury did not occur on our property" or "He was not on staff; he was just a volunteer." Each of these is an attempt to manage the impressions others are forming of the apologizer.

3. *"This is not in accordance with our values."* Apologies often include attempts to dissociate the behavior from what the apologizer wants others to believe is their typical conduct. They might admit responsibility for the harm but fear that admission will create a permanent link between them and the wrong behavior. They want the offense to be seen as an outlier, an aberration that is unlikely to be observed under normal circumstances. For example, institutions have defended their exposed leader by drawing attention to how that leader was under stress, medicated, or impaired in some way and could therefore not function normally.

4. *"Had I known then what I know now, I would have made a different decision."* This apoloscuse denies having the foresight, training, or competency needed to avoid the harmful behavior. The apologizer quickly

follows their admission of responsibility with an acknowledgment of ignorance. Often the apologizer fails to acknowledge whether they *should* have known or had the opportunity to know but chose to look the other way. In the church I worked at, I came across numerous individuals in positions of authority who deliberately chose not to look at the evidence I made available to them. At one point a leader told me, "I don't think I should look at this." I was devastated. It is hard enough to not be believed. It is harder still to know you will not even be heard. So when one of those leaders publicly claimed, "I never knew any of this," while not disclosing the deliberate choice not to know, he was deceiving the audience in the hope that they would accept his apoloscuse. And that is often precisely what happens. People who want to believe the best respond by saying, "Don't be too hard on yourself. How could you have known? You can't be expected to fix a problem you do not know exists."

5. *"It was outside my authority to control."* This is seen in institutional settings where the wrongdoer claims they were just following orders or that they didn't have the authority to intervene. Many have been injured by those who were willing to sacrifice another's well-being and their own integrity in order to maintain a position, income, or sense of peace. Primo Levi, a Holocaust survivor, wrote of his

experience at Auschwitz, "Monsters exist, but they are too few in number to be truly dangerous; more dangerous are the common men, the functionaries ready to believe and to act without asking questions."[3]

The Concession That Justifies

The concession that implies you deserved harm, or that you are complicit because you didn't do more to prevent it, is perhaps the most damaging of all the pseudo-apologies. It says, "I'm sorry, but you aren't innocent either." It suggests the harm would not have happened had you not acted in a certain way. Parents who mistreat and abuse their children use these justifications, as do husbands who inflict violence upon their wives, and authority figures who intimidate and coerce their subordinates. The apology that justifies can also place the focus on the harm itself and suggest that you are making too much of it. "I'm sorry, but I don't see what the big deal is." They could even suggest that the harm they caused will, in the end, prove to be good for you—perhaps you learned some valuable lessons or formed qualities like strength and resilience.

There are, of course, legitimate excuses and justifications. A person who accidentally hits another car should not suffer the same consequences as someone who intentionally rams another vehicle. However, an apology is not the appropriate context for a defense. I've found that when I keep an apology focused entirely on the harm caused by my behavior, then the other person is more open to, and perhaps will even request, an explanation as to what went wrong. An apology takes on a different purpose whenever it becomes a defense.

The Concession That Self-Promotes

Brenda and Sandy had been good friends for nearly five years, but Brenda was becoming increasingly concerned with the control Sandy had over her life. Brenda felt like she needed to run every significant decision by Sandy. Brenda always feared how Sandy might respond if she went against her advice. Now she was confronting Sandy about it and asking for more space. At first, Sandy denied that she was trying to control Brenda's life in any way. She became agitated, saying, "If you don't want my help, then don't ask me." But Brenda continued to provide example after example of how Sandy had crossed boundaries. Finally, Sandy relented. She muttered the words, "I'm sorry," and then spent the next fifteen minutes recounting all the good things she had ever done for Brenda.

The person preoccupied with their image will typically promote themselves while attempting to apologize, as Sandy did. These self-promotions usually appear near the end of the apology, as if the person apologizing knows they are losing control and must lay claim to their legitimacy before they finish the apology. Many public statements of apology put out by organizations or leaders quickly become pitches for why they are still worthy of continued support and engagement from their followers. They acknowledge the past

Many public statements of apology quickly become pitches for why organizations or leaders are still worthy of continued support from their followers.

wrongs while still wanting to be seen as incapable of future wrongdoing.

A statement of apology should never double as a medal. For example, acknowledgment of institutional abuses tends to come with assurances that the institution and their leaders are on the same side as the victims, even though their actions have demonstrated the opposite. This is a fear-based response that concerns itself with how the victims and their supporters view the organization. But one of the most significant ways to honor victims is to recognize their agency—their freedom to form their own opinions. The victims should be the ones to decide whether or not the organization is on their side and be given the space needed to determine whether promises of change will be kept.

The Concession That Asks for Sympathy

Mark was nervous as he began to address the faculty members who had gathered to hear from him. He was the president of a small liberal arts college that had hired a since-removed provost who took a slash-and-burn approach to programming with little regard for those whose jobs were being removed. Mark was promised quick and sudden growth and was so starstruck by the charisma of the provost that he ignored the initial reports of abusive power. He had seen the red flags all along and had even envisioned such a worst-case scenario when he recommended the provost. Now he was attempting to keep his own job: "I've never gone through a situation so difficult as this. I've laid awake at night wondering what I could have done differently. I'm sorry. I know many of you are hurting. I'm hurting too. These have been the hardest months of my life."

The apology that asks for sympathy says, "I'm hurting too." I'm amazed at how often the ones who have caused the harm will displace the pain of the wounded with the pain of the wounder. Each of these pleas, promotions, justifications, excuses, appeals, and condemnations reveal an inability on the part of the apologizer to get outside themselves, which is a necessary prerequisite to any apology. Such messages should have no place within an apology and only serve to reorient compassion.

An Apology SCORE Card

When any concession tactic shows up in an "apology," it is normal to question the sincerity of the apologizer, especially when dealing with a narcissistic and abusive manipulator. To help discern whether an individual or organization has given an authentic apology, use the following SCORE card. It is in no way comprehensive—relationships and the dynamics that sustain them are complex. Just as we can't always create blueprints that tell us precisely what to do and how to do it, apologies ought to be highly contextualized. However, this SCORE card does provide a helpful check for those who are attempting to apologize—or those who are on the receiving end of a deceptive apology.

Does the apology . . .

☐ **S—SURRENDER**
Give up the desire to defend? ("I owe you an apology . . .")

☐ **C—CONFESSION**
Rightly name each wrong to acknowledge fully what has been done? ("I was wrong when I . . .")

☐ **O—OWNERSHIP**
Acknowledge the active role they had had in the wrongdoing? ("I take complete responsibility for . . .")

☐ **R—RECOGNITION**
Specifically state the harm caused by the wrongdoing? ("I see how my actions caused you . . .")

☐ **E—EMPATHY**
Make a true connection with the weight of what has been done? ("I am grieved and filled with remorse . . .")

Surrender. The hardest step in the process of an authentic apology is giving up the desire to defend. We feel this even in our smallest disputes, don't we? Whether it's a quibble at work or a fight between spouses, no one wants to surrender their side; no one wants to feel the shame of being wrong. Similarly, when I analyze statements of institutional apology, surrender is hard to come by. I often observe what remains when every blame, excuse, justification, and self-promotion is crossed out. At times, nothing remains. In most cases, one or two sentences of acknowledgment and remorse are all that is left. These statements typically address the wrong in vague and general terms—such as "We condemn abuse in every form"—but do not go so far as to identify the specific actions they took and the decisions they made. And rather than address specific harms that specific individuals experienced, they decry such types of wrongs in general: "We grieve anytime someone is abused." It's easier to "apologize" for a hypothetical wound experienced by nameless victims. Many are just unwilling to surrender their defenses and promotions.

Confession. Surrender paves the way for confession. I believe each wrong must be rightly named, a true acknowledgment of what has occurred. A confession starts with the words "We were wrong when . . ." The statement serves as a mirror that reflects back to the wounded all the actions that hurt them, a mirror that too often victims have to hold up themselves. In some cases, the confession might need to become more than just a mirror that reflects what is known to be wrong and instead be a spotlight that acknowledges both known and unknown wrongs. Many sexual offenders, for example, have only confessed to the abuses that have been exposed. A truly repentant person will confess other hidden abuses that need to be brought into the light. Surrendered people likely give a number of confessions that match or exceed the number of truths presented in the exposure.

Surrendered people likely give a number of confessions that match or exceed the number of truths presented in the exposure.

Confession may require a period of listening or inviting an investigation first. If an individual or an organization is serious about confession, they won't avoid a truth-seeking process, because they know that healing is impossible until the wounds are properly assessed. Confession is shortchanged as long as the truth remains undiscovered. A person in pain might go to a doctor and say, "Doctor, the problem seems to be in my neck." The doctor, however, will not just accept the patient's diagnosis (hopefully!). Rather, they will conduct their own assessment using the tools, education, and experience that their expertise affords them. The doctor may then say to the patient, "While the pain is in your neck, the source of the problem is in your back." Confession simply says, "Here's what I know to be wrong."

Ownership. The abusive person or organization must also acknowledge their active role. Passive apologies like "Mistakes were made" seek to avoid shame by avoiding ownership. Those in the wrong should take ownership by saying something like, "I take complete and full responsibility for . . ." Another way a person can demonstrate ownership is by inviting, accepting, or imposing consequences on themselves. For example, a person who commits a crime might turn themselves in to the police as if to say, "I am willing to accept the consequences for what I've done." Similarly, an organization's leadership will often make necessary changes in leadership once they own up to the wrongs they've committed.

Recognition. Out of ownership should flow recognition. Just as specific wrongs were named, specific harms should also be identified. The apologizer says, "I recognize that my actions resulted in . . ." If confession and ownership say, "I acknowledge the illegitimacy of my actions," recognition says, "And I will take upon myself the shame my actions produced."

It is at this point in an authentic apology that the scope and severity of the abuse are laid bare. The wounded and their wounds are faced instead of shunned. Remaining is a solitary bridge across which the offender must walk and with vulnerability say, "I will claim the shame I've asked you to carry but was always mine to begin with, and I will surrender the legitimacy I've tried to claim but was always yours from the start." What a powerful moment.

Empathy. Once the individual or organization has finally absorbed the truth of their wrongdoing and the gravity of their wrongs, then they will feel the weight of the hurt and the shame, know they are defenseless and at the mercy of others, and must begin the difficult work of restitution and restoration. They feel it. And out of that broken place of surrender, confession, ownership, recognition, and empathy might emerge the words, "I am so very sorry."

* * *

Six months after my resignation from the church where I worked, I received an invitation to return to hear a public apology from the board. I was stunned. I never foresaw such a day. I was also wary. Were they only doing this because of the pressure they were feeling after their exposure? They sent me a copy of the apology they planned to read. It was much more comprehensive than I expected. Also, one of the elders, a longtime ally of the senior pastor, had resigned over the decision to apologize publicly. I saw this as a sign that the others were willing to do what was right. So my wife and I returned to the church.

We arrived as people were making their way in and out of the auditorium after the morning services, quietly took our seats in the first row, and waited anxiously for the meeting to begin. The elders walked onto the platform together, and then the chairman read the apology. As I listened to his words, it felt as if a weight of shame was lifted from my shoulders. They took responsibility for their actions, and they owned the shame those actions caused—not in a way that caused me to look upon them with condemnation, but in a way that felt just and dignified. We were relieved that the truth was out at last.

What that board did is what I believe most are unwilling to do—to reclaim the shame from those they have blamed. Shame, when owned by those who are supposed to be above reproach, carries consequences. In this case, the elders did the right thing by invoking penalties on themselves. Many people avoid shame because they know it will result in some form of loss—a loss of the very things they've worked to obtain and perhaps are now clinging to for meaning. But it is only through a willingness to surrender, confess, own, recognize, and empathize that an apology has the capacity to be a freeing and healing moment for the victim who has been wronged.

CHAPTER 7 SUMMARY

CONCESSIONS

When it's clear that abuse has happened, an abusive person or organization may offer an apology to the person harmed. But sometimes
those apologies are merely concessions—statements made to avoid
a scandal rather than a genuine apology that is intended to heal and
restore. There are several kinds of concessions: concessions that
condemn, appease, excuse, justify, self-promote, ask for sympathy.

ANATOMY OF A CONCESSION THAT . . .

CONDEMNS

The apologizer is unwilling to acknowledge their wrongs and instead
argues that the fault lies with the person who is feeling wronged.

APPEASES

The apologizer is simply trying to appease the demands of
someone with greater power rather than righting a wrong.

EXCUSES

The apologizer believes that extenuating circumstances diminish
their blame.

JUSTIFIES

The apologizer implies that you were complicit in the wrong or
deserved the wrong in some way.

SELF-PROMOTES

The apologizer uses the apology as an opportunity to highlight
their good attributes.

ASKS FOR SYMPATHY

The apologizer shifts attention to their own hurt while offering an
apology to another.

CHAPTER 8

DEMONSTRATIONS

A megachurch was reeling after news broke of the pastor's abusive behavior. For years, he had been ruling his staff like an oppressive leader, acting rashly and without regard for those he said were "family." There were even rumors he made unwanted advances toward women on the team, forcing them to keep their mouths shut if they wanted to keep their jobs. The board was previously made aware of the abuse and conducted their own investigation, but they decided to clear the pastor of wrongdoing. Now, the entire leadership was facing a threat to its image.

They were in crisis mode. Regrettably, their focus remained solely on what this latest exposure would do to *them* rather than what the abuse and deception had done to the *victims*. Meetings lasted into the night as they strategized with their legal and public relations teams to determine how they could avoid liability, maintain giving, and ameliorate public concerns. One board member proposed "flushing the system" with good reports. "We need to regain the trust of the people by showing them that good things are still happening," they said. "After all, lives are being changed. People are still being baptized. God is not finished with us."

That was it—the plan was formed. The church quickly launched a campaign to demonstrate their goodwill: e-mail blasts contained stories of outreach to the community, mission efforts overseas, and testimonies of changed lives, and the pastoral team encouraged their people to keep giving, showing up, and supporting God's work. Peppered throughout all communication were reassuring phrases, some of the other pastors even going so far as to offer their own stories of commitment to the church: "My family continues to give. We've even increased our tithe because we so believe in this place."

The people of the church loved it. Especially after so much drama, they liked being reassured that the place they had invested in was what they hoped and imagined it would be. While the church continued to deliver a steady stream of messages about the good work they were doing, it did seem like messages about the abuses and how the leadership was addressing their failures seemed to be few and far between, but that was okay—it was time to move on. It was a leadership issue, so the leaders should be trusted to handle it. Many people stopped reading any updates that were sent out in regard to the "situation." After all, the best days were still ahead.

If you've been the victim of church hurt or spiritual abuse, it's likely that the above scene feels uncannily familiar. The abuse you endured was finally brought to light, but instead of an authentic apology, it felt like you got the opposite: an insincere concession followed by a barrage of displays and reassurances that the church was still good and *thriving*. These demonstrations of change and goodwill are a common tactic for any offending party. By drawing attention to successes, the good done since the exposure, or the positive influence on the community, the abusive person or organization demonstrates to a watching world that they deserve to possess what they want. What they want, of course, is continued control and reputation. By drowning a negative event in a sea of positivity, the organization manipulates its stakeholders into overlooking or justifying wrongs. It's terribly effective because the people ultimately conclude, "Let's not be concerned about one drop of bad in a sea of good."

It's true: we should be discerning and supportive of good-faith efforts. But it's equally important not to blindly accept the mirage they offer. Whenever an organization apologizes for its unethical behavior but then goes on to promote its values, successes, and contributions to society, you can be sure it is more interested in repairing its image for its own benefit than it is in making amends for the good of the wronged.

When organizations
devote greater urgency
to demonstrating change
than to pursuing an
understanding of the problems,
they sacrifice truth.

And like many of the tactics we've discussed in this book, demonstrations carry the potential of long-term harm for the community. We must understand that potential—as well as the intricacies of these appealing demonstrations—before we can be fully empowered and equipped to speak truth to power.

The Danger of Demonstrations

Because these demonstrations are based on deception and designed to protect the abuser's image, they present a dangerous false hope that can do great damage to a person's religious faith, trust in others, and hope for justice. When a church, for example, asks people to continue to have faith—"God's not finished with us yet" or "We have more to offer this world"—and then fails to deliver on their promises, their failure can weaken people's faith, if not destroy it.

This is the tragedy of demonstrations of change without regard for truth. They lead to a superficial treatment of people's brokenness. When organizations devote greater urgency to demonstrating change than to pursuing an understanding of the problems that caused the need for change, they sacrifice truth. And this has serious consequences. At best, this allows blind spots in the organization to remain. At worst, the "change" is a form of stagecraft used to maintain favor with an audience. To borrow a biblical phrase, the community claims, "Peace!" when there is no peace. They desire to be seen as good without having to meet the demands of goodness. They want to be granted trust without having to earn it. They want to be seen as agents of healing without repairing any wounds. They want to collect a following without stopping to serve those they've trampled over.

We reinforce these behaviors when we reward them. The last step in the cover-up of dark secrets is convincing others to endorse the demonstrations as evidence of real change. Victims, pushed to the margins, are left to watch the victory of hypocrisy. At this point, there is nothing left for them to do. They've done what they could, and it wasn't enough. Sure, it might not mark the end of the story; future exposure might be possible through another opportunity to speak out, or from new testimonies. But the waiting will be difficult and damaging, adding further trauma to the already traumatized.

It is very difficult to discern these final acts of deception. In this respect, they are similar to the charms I described at the beginning of this book. Demonstrations are used to win your favor, and because they appear good, you naturally want to believe they are free of hidden agendas. And because you've likely been through a difficult crisis, it will be tempting to welcome and support a demonstration that signals a new beginning. I want to encourage you to remain discerning and willing to confront abuse so you do not fall for the final ploy.

And if you have been enabling abuse, or are a part of a community or an organization in crisis, I want to encourage you that you still have the power to stand with victims and advocate for truth. You can choose not to celebrate a demonstration of change if an actual change hasn't followed truth telling. You can choose to voice your concern and call the powerful to do the right thing. You can dissent, even if it might seem as if everyone else is ready to applaud the demonstrations. It is never too late to speak the truth about a wrong that was never made right.

Decoding Demonstrations

Demonstrations come in various forms. Many involve highlighting principles, values, policies, and promises. Demonstrations are deceptions that divert attention from the negativity of the harm and toward the positivity of well-sounding statements and philanthropic actions.

Statements

If accusations of abuse involve crimes against society, it is common for an organization or individual to respond with a demonstration that includes a plethora of prosocial statements that align with societal values. These statements condemn abusive behavior and highlight best practices, renewed commitments, and future potential. Many of the statements I've analyzed read something like this:

> We are so thankful for the courage of all true
> victims who have come forward and commend their
> commitment to seeking justice for the abused. Like
> so many, we are grieved and angered whenever we

hear that someone has been abused. It is why we
make sure all of our staff and volunteers undergo a
rigorous vetting process that includes background
checks and abuse-awareness training. We take
seriously our duty to care for those who are part of
our community. At the same time, we must protect
ourselves from those who continue to sow discord
by mischaracterizing us to the public. One only has
to look at our record of supporting the marginalized
and the oppressed to understand that we would
never knowingly subject others to the injustices some
are still accusing us of. We will continue to do all we
can to earn your trust.

This statement makes it seem like the organization sides
with victims. They express gratitude for the victims' courage
but seem to want the reader to know there are two categories
of victims: true and false. Embedded in this distinction is the
implication that the victims bringing the accusations are not
"true" victims—they are either lying, confused, or somehow
deserve the harm. It's a small distinction that I've consistently
observed across cases involving a cover-up. Victims have been
told they are not "true victims" as a result of this distinction,
like one man who told his story of being abused as a teenager
by an adult woman and subsequently heard those closest to
him say he can't claim to be a "true victim" since he was big-
ger and stronger than the woman at the time of the abuse.
Going back to the statement above, the organization then

demonstrates their prosocial values: "like so many . . ." They want to be seen as on the same side as a serious and caring society. The supposed evidence of this is their vetting process and abuse training. Finally, they demonstrate their history of supporting marginalized groups as a reason why the accusations should be dismissed outright. Rather than consider the merits of the accusation itself, or commission an independent investigation, they seek to offer demonstrations of their own values, procedures, and history as the only evidence the public should need.

Distancing

The abuser might promise to never harm again, offering assurances that the abusive behavior was very unlike them. The exposed person who emphasizes how long ago the abuse was is attempting to create distance between who they were then and who they are now. We tend to care more about recent harm. By highlighting a gap in time, the offender implies that the actions are in the distant past. They might then compare an isolated incident to all the good behavior they have otherwise demonstrated. By crowding the space between then and now with examples of positive behavior, the exposed individual seeks to demonstrate why people should not be concerned.

This is the tactic Mike used when a woman he sexually assaulted twenty years ago at a college party came forward and shared her abuse with a journalist. After the story ran,

Mike quickly pointed out that the incident occurred more than twenty years ago. He convinced many of his friends and followers to write public letters of support on social media. People began sharing stories of the good things he had done for them over the years. He was unwilling to acknowledge, however, that his crime was never reported, that he had never faced justice, and that the victim had been living with a terrible secret for twenty years. He only wanted people to believe that all his good works since have atoned for that one "dark moment."

Rehab

Other demonstrations include abusers' focused attempts to engage in new behaviors and participate in new activities as a way of rehabilitating themselves. Often the offender using this type of demonstration purely as a tactic to win favor will insist on controlling the rehabilitation process. They will refuse to submit to someone else's plan. They then promote their healing process as a reason to be trusted and accepted again. Similarly, an individual might go out of their way to buy a gift or do something sacrificial for the person they've hurt. An organization might hold an awareness-raising event, develop educational materials, and give the issues where they've fallen short a focus at upcoming conferences and meetings. However, if these self-governed rehabilitation efforts are driven by a desire to win back acceptance in the least painful way possible, then they will be temporary. The demonstrations will disappear from view as quickly as they entered into focus. Most will be satisfied, but the victimized and the vulnerable will still be left wondering if they can trust again. As time passes, and as more and more people accept the demonstrations, they sense that others are leaving them behind. This allows patterns of self-blame and condemnation to reemerge. *Is something wrong with me for wanting more? Am I being too hard on them? Am I expecting too much?* Those in the wrong do not stop to see where the wounded are. Instead, they believe they can move on now that the demonstrations are over.

Telltale Signs

Once you are able to identify that what you are seeing is a demonstration tactic, you can look closer and see the heart of the individual or organization between the lines: narrow-mindedness, arrogance, and an insistence on leading are telltale signs the demonstration of change is only for the sake of repairing an image, not a genuine change. They will do only what is needed to survive the scandal instead of doing all they must to make amends. They will be unwilling to consider all the factors that might have contributed to their abusive behavior when pushed. They alone will determine what is up for discussion and what is not.

Many who simply want to demonstrate their right to continue to have power will act out of an overconfidence in their understanding of the wounds and what is needed for healing.

Individuals or organizations using demonstration tactics will do only what is needed to survive the scandal instead of doing all they must to make amends.

We see this dynamic often in abusive relationships. An abusive person who has harmed others insists that they—and they alone—know best what is needed to achieve a different future. They want to be the sole authority able to diagnose what happened and what needs to change. And since they are the one giving the diagnosis, they are also the one prescribing the treatment. The abusive person might rationalize this by saying, "I need to be able to figure this out on my own. I'm in charge. I know myself better than anyone. I just need time and space."

We see exactly the same thing happening in organizational settings. The overconfident will shun outside help from experts because they believe they already know what they need to know—how could someone from the outside be more of an expert? Concerned only about appearances, they refuse to engage with outsiders who might inform their initiatives and expose any blind spots. They stay far away from those who might reveal their limitations. Trusting in their own ability to investigate claims and to render judgment, they go on their own fact-finding missions and refuse to hire outside, nonbiased investigators. At the same time, they avoid giving any credibility to the power of public opinion—to those who have exposed them. Such acknowledgment would give the perception that they do not know what they are doing, an admission they perceive to be fatal and one that would simultaneously give credit to the effectiveness of the public outcry, which they fear would empower their critics even more. They have now entered into a cycle of impression management as they feel they must defend their legitimacy at every turn so as to quell the growing concerns. But some people on the receiving end of these messages, perhaps members of an organization or the public, are not so easily convinced and rightly become increasingly concerned by the organization's stubbornness.

It takes great courage to be one of those people not so easily convinced. Because what happens when the organization's quest to positively influence public perception does not end with the success they had hoped for? They turn their attention to managing the impressions others are forming of the critics, labeling them as malicious, hateful, and arrogant. The deceived who support the organization's efforts then condemn those they are led to believe are worse than they really are. Sadly, the very people who were repeatedly ignored are now publicly scorned. The quest to qualify themselves has now become a quest to disqualify others. The same dynamic can be seen in our interpersonal relationships. The abusive person who insists on leading their own change might eventually attack you for insisting that they get help. "Who do you think you are? You aren't any better than me. You have problems too, you know. Why don't you focus on yourself and leave me be?"

But What Can I Do?

There are some responses available to you if you believe the person or organization is attempting to pull the fleece over your eyes with a demonstration. One response is to just wait. If you aren't sure the person is sincere, allow time to be the test. If they grow impatient with you or pressure you into praising their efforts, then that might be an indicator that they are only interested in your acceptance. Because demonstrations tend to come and go, whereas authentic change has a lasting effect, waiting it out can be an alternative to blindly accepting a demonstration.

If you have the opportunity and means to be more direct, and it is safe to do so, then you can try pointing the person or organization back to the wrongs that haven't been made known or made right. You might say something like "While I can understand your desire to show me how you are changing, I still don't believe you have looked at everything that went wrong. I'm concerned you have not done the work needed to understand your responsibility for the hurt you caused." Because demonstrations seek to distract, a practical way to counter that effort is to keep pointing back to the unresolved issues.

The mere fact that some wrongs have not been amended or certain truths have not yet been uncovered does not necessarily mean the steps toward change are being taken with the wrong motive. This is why discernment is important. You want to support a sincere desire to grow and change. Perhaps they simply do not see what they still need to do. However, the person or organization engaging in good-faith efforts will listen to those who call them back to a process of uncovering truth and righting wrongs. If they respond in a way that produces trust instead of fear, then their actions, even if premature, are more likely driven by a desire for truth than a desire to deceive.

But What If They've Really Changed?

It's understandable that you—as a victim of abuse or as a member of a community where abuse has occurred—want to believe the best about those in power, and even more that you want to believe and hope for true and authentic change in their hearts. This is why you must use the above information to be extremely discerning whenever you're faced with a demonstrative response that promises that everything will be different. Because here's the unfortunate truth: no amount of patience will produce change in an abusive community that isn't willing to surrender its legitimacy and pursue the entire truth. No amount of faith will be rewarded when the object of that faith is a falsehood. And after the dust settles and the crisis has abated, will the community have succeeded in becoming a safer place? How can they when they have yet to turn to the truth?

If they have any hope of being a refuge for the vulnerable, a model for others to follow, and a source of healing, then they must first be willing to confront themselves before they confront others. They must search high and low for the abuses and abusers in their midst, encourage their people to report known or suspected crimes to the police, and courageously remove the abusers from their positions of power. Only then will their service to others be communicated with the clarity of sincere truth. Only then will their words and actions be backed by the persuasiveness of truth and integrity.

CHAPTER 8 SUMMARY

DEMONSTRATIONS

Once an abuse is brought to light, an abusive person or organization will offer concessions and then demonstrations to reassure others that the abuse is in the past. These demonstrations can be dangerous if they are insincere and are employed merely as a way to protect an abuser's image or to keep an abuser in power. Demonstrations come in various forms: statements, distancing, and rehabilitation. Demonstrations seek to repair an image rather than engage in genuine change.

STATEMENTS

Statements offer a version of the story that display an alignment with prosocial values. They are designed to downplay abuse and highlight the abusive person or organization's commitment to safety and care for others.

DISTANCING

The abuser might promise to never harm again, offering assurances that the abusive behavior was very unlike them. Distancing can highlight the passage of time or the good that a person has done to demonstrate that the abusive behavior was a lapse or an aberration.

REHABILITATION

Rehabilitation attempts to demonstrate an abuser's focused attempt to engage in new behaviors and participate in new activities as a way of reforming themselves.

CHAPTER 9

WHAT NOW?

You may have picked up this book unsure of how to describe your own experience. If you've read through these tactics and realize you are living through them right now, I encourage you to consider speaking to someone, like a licensed therapist, who can help you unravel the threads. Your story matters. You have the right to tell it. And it might just begin a process of healing.

After years of enduring confusion and oppressive leadership, I finally began to crack. I was so weary. God and my marriage received only whatever leftover energy I had at the end of each day—and it wasn't enough. I wanted to believe I could hold it all together, but the seams were bursting. In an effort to find a way to protect ourselves from the toxicity of our church situation and reset our relationship, my wife and I decided to travel and meet with an older couple who we knew mentored church leaders, specifically those who were encountering difficult ministry issues.

It ended up being one of the most pivotal weekends in my healing journey. Though I certainly had been processing my experience with my wife and close friends, it was the first time I shared what had happened—and how it was affecting me and my family—with someone who was outside the situation. When I finished, they said, "It is clear to us you've never been given the opportunity to tell your story, and we wanted to give the space to do that." Telling our story over the course of that entire morning was at once difficult and freeing. Our pain, although hard to speak of, was heard by those who were not threatened by it. They didn't try to rush us through it or over it, and that made all the difference in the world.

I think many live with untold stories, not because they never want to tell them, but because they never encounter safe people and safe places where their stories can be heard.

As you've read through each abuse tactic in this book, you may have recognized your situation in some of them, ways you've been hurt and taken advantage of by a person or an organization you once thought you could trust. The grief of awareness can be extremely overwhelming as you confront and acknowledge these wounds, maybe for the first time. My greatest prayer is that, alongside that very valid grief,

Many live with untold stories, not because they never want to tell them, but because they never encounter safe people and safe places where their stories can be heard.

there would also be a glimmer of hope—the hope that you have the beginning of a language to describe your experience, to bring the darkness into the light. Whether with a close confidant or a licensed therapist, finding the space to safely tell your story of abuse is the first step in your healing journey. Telling our story to someone else didn't provide all the answers for how to resolve the situation we were in, but it did open the door to our own hearts. It allowed each of us to ask questions like *Who am I being as I go through this? What effects is it having on me? How am I treating those closest to me? How do I avoid becoming what I'm condemning? How do I function above the dysfunction?*

Advocating for yourself does not come without effort and pain. You won't simply leave the house of abuse and walk into a house of freedom down the road. Recovery might force you to revisit the ruins left by the abuser. This is difficult. Sometimes I think I can just leave the broken pieces behind me and move on. People come along and say, "Forgive and forget." But healing sometimes means going back to find every jagged edge and sharp corner of what has been broken. And as you do, you work through what must be done to restore what has been broken. Much of that restoration will be outside of your control, but it helps to know what is ideal, even if it is seemingly impossible. Only then can you know what to ask for if you ever get the opportunity.

And the good news is, as you reconstruct your sense of self-worth and self-respect, you try new things, explore new perspectives, and form new and healthier views of yourself and the world around you. You are reoriented around what is truly valuable in this life. Your focus is restored, and reality comes into view.

The Principle of Opposite Action

But are there things you can do right now to begin resisting these tactics of manipulation and control? What I've described in this book is a pattern: a hidden language of abuse that must be decoded in order to find freedom from its power. Once it is decoded, then you can identify it and name it. Once you can name it, then you can call it out.

In addition to learning the language of abuse and beginning to confide your story to a trusted individual, there are ways that you can resist abuse and advocate for yourself within your situation. After all, once you can fully admit and understand the depth of abuse you've been experiencing, it doesn't mean that everything magically fixes itself. Yet small steps make great changes, and what's important is that you begin.

Reframe

Because abuse breeds in secrecy, confronting it is doing the opposite of what it wants you to do: confronting abuse is seeing it when it wants you to look away; making sense of what you are facing when it wants you to accept confusion; opposing it when it wants you to remain converted; speaking when it wants you to be silent. Confronting is *choosing*. More than anything, abuse takes away your agency—your ability to choose for yourself. Finding that agency is an important step toward freedom and recovery. Certainly, there will still be fear—for me, every decision I made after speaking out against our church leadership was fraught with fear. But I cannot describe the depth of freedom I felt when I finally started to advocate for myself.

Knowing that the abusive person or organization wants to control your perception of them, it can be helpful to ask yourself, *What does the abuser want me to do?* whenever you begin to feel manipulated. Once you've identified that (and it's not always clear), then the next question is, *What would be the opposite action?* If the answer to that question is clear, and the action is feasible and ethical, then one way you can resist an abuser's manipulation is to do the opposite of what they're telling you to do. That is the process of reframing, of using your agency to regain control of the situation.

When you start to exercise your voice and agency, those who would prefer you to stay silent and powerless might try to use your past trauma against you by suggesting you still have a lot of healing to do, are clouded by bitterness, are emotionally unhealthy, and so forth. They want you to doubt yourself and stand down. Knowing that, doing the opposite would then be to believe in yourself and stand up. Your past might actually be the reason you see so clearly now, insist on fairness, and get rightly upset over injustice.

The principle of opposite action isn't simply doing the

opposite of what evil is doing but doing the opposite of what evil wants *you* to do. Abuse continues to unfurl until it covers the entire space of your life. It is an enveloping darkness, a spreading cancer, and an ever-expanding web of tangled threads. Freedom comes when the abuse is rolled back. It means the darkness is receding, the cancer is in remission, and each thread that binds is being cut away. You advocate for yourself with each step of opposition, however small that step might be.

It's important to keep in mind that opposition is not simple, and it's not always safe: you will not suddenly and easily become an opposer of abuse after a long time of functioning under an abuser's control. Your whole world has been dismantled—it takes time to process that trauma and rebuild your life. Depending on the severity of your situation, you might also need to come up with a safety plan with the help of an advocacy center or professional. For those of us who are advocating for the abused, may we remember not to push people through this necessary work and not to neglect their need for safety. We must honor and protect their agency and safety in the same way we cherish our own, gently speaking the truth and allowing each person to decide for themselves what they will do with what they hear.

Cultivate Beauty

I still find myself in personally abusive situations, but I see more clearly now, and I am less afraid. Many have asked me

Recovery is like taking
a feature that by itself
is ugly and unwanted
but is repurposed
when placed within
a larger context of beauty.

how I protect myself from vicarious trauma or from becoming overly despairing and cynical. My answer: I look for and cultivate beauty.

Every act of abuse is an assault on beauty, so I've learned to find the beauty the abuser is seeking to assault and dismantle. I try to appreciate the life that has been ruined while not ignoring the anger I feel over the devastation. That means I must slow down as I come into contact with an abusive situation and allow myself to hear what the injustice is communicating.

I've also learned to see and cultivate the beauty in my everyday life. I oppose evil whenever I cultivate the growth of what it wants to destroy. For me, this beauty is found in the relationships I've formed—in the laughter around a table of friends, in the tears shared between bearers of pain, and in the songs that reflect the values of a community. It's in the joy of the friendship my wife and I share with each other and in every facet of our life together as a growing family. It's in the church we left—not in the building, but in the people. Even as I write this, I'm looking forward to returning to the church in less than a day from now to celebrate the wedding of someone dear to us.

I've learned to see more of the beauty in the natural world as well and to pay more attention to the wonder all around. Each spring I spend hours planting hundreds of flowers. I'm a novice for sure, but something about the planting, pruning, and watering of a garden brings life, and each year I learn new methods for cultivating the beauty in nature. Gardening has taught me lessons about growing in the midst of pain. Healing isn't as easy as replacing old ground with new territory. We have to work with what we have, and some roots and structures are not going anywhere, so we learn to grow beauty around them. Recovery is like that. It's not a strict replacement of parts—a new piece in place of the broken piece. It's more like taking a feature that by itself is ugly and unwanted but is repurposed when placed within a larger context of beauty.

Seeing and cultivating beauty also has preventative powers. The more acquainted you become with authentic beauty, the more quickly you can identify fraudulent beauty. You can sense that something's not right because you have a better sense of what *is* right.

And that's when you can become a true advocate for change.

Building a Safe Community

Abuse is not someone else's personal and private matter that we can ignore out of a concern for minding our own business, nor is it a matter to be only attended to by a select few in leadership positions. Abuse is a community concern. Therefore, the question must be asked of each of us: *In what ways am I perpetuating an abusive culture through my silence or tacit endorsement of those who are in the wrong?* It is not a question of simple beliefs or values but a question of practice. Practically speaking, what kind of people should we be once a secret is out? Do we ignore what is behind the curtain because we want the show to go on? How long do we continue to provide abusers with the very things they use deception to gain? Do we keep handing them our money? Keep sitting at their feet? Keep following their lead? Is all the grief over the abuse simply to end in strong statements of condemnation, conferences, and prayers? Is there nothing that can be done, as well as said? What can we expect, beyond words, that can assure us of the sincerity of the community's newfound resolve to end abuse? One action might surpass them all. And it is this: to open all the windows of the darkened house until every nook and cranny is covered in light so that all the damage can be seen. It is to surrender to that light, even if it means there will be no possibility of retaining or regaining legitimacy. It is to put every possible contributing factor on the table for inspection, even the system itself, and to be willing to recognize that perhaps it cannot be fixed and that something new must be created in its place.

Recall the image I presented in chapter 5 of the lamb caught in a thicket who does not receive the help it needs from the shepherds walking by. It's not just the powerful friends and allies of the abuser who often fail to reach into the thicket to rescue the lamb. Those of us who come to learn of the plight of the victim must consider our own responsibility in that moment. When we hear the cry of the victim and the deceptive pleas of the abuser—are we honest and sincere about who we choose to gather around and why? Our response reveals whose voice we honor more. Consider these words from Judith Herman: "It is very tempting to take the side of the perpetrator. All the perpetrator asks is that the bystander do nothing. He appeals to the universal desire to see, hear, and speak no evil. The victim, on the contrary, asks the bystander to share the burden of pain. The victim demands action, engagement, and remembering."[1]

People often defend their silence by saying, "I don't want to take sides." More often than not, that is simply an excuse for not pursuing truth. Who do we usually hear that from? The leadership attempting to maintain order. And even after the truth has been established, those who chose not to pursue the truth often want to remain neutral. But there is no remaining neutral. Bystanders must take sides, either to be active supporters of the wounded or to actively turn their backs. There is only deception and truth. People who choose to remain neutral are giving safe passage to lies. Elie Wiesel powerfully said, "I swore never to be silent whenever and wherever human beings endure suffering and humiliation. We must take sides. Neutrality helps the oppressor, never the victim. Silence encourages the tormenter, never the tormented."[2]

A practical way that bystanders can support victims through action is by calling the community to conduct an independent investigation, allowing an outside group of trained, trauma-informed professionals to unearth what is buried and present what is true. When crimes are involved, this investigation should be led by law enforcement. Outside investigators, whether law enforcement or other professionals, can help an organization define the problem accurately.

Sometimes supporting the victim means immediately withdrawing support from those who have yet to speak the truth about the abuse and refuse to allow light to shine. This might seem harsh or an overreaction, but consider what it communicates to the watching victims when they see people gathering around the people who wounded them—to see them giving money to the institution, using their services, applauding their efforts, and endorsing their legitimacy. Consider also what it communicates to the public. Your participation signals to others that this is a safe place.

Elizabeth Heyrick believes that "we furnish the stimulant to . . . injustice . . . by purchasing its produce."[3] I agree. Many people want to continue to enjoy what the abusive community produces—things like teachings, works of art, or services. By doing so, they provide the nourishment that the abusive community needs to grow stronger. It will continue to line its pockets with the profits, continue to lead with fists that harm, and continue to invent lies with its tongue. Sometimes a decision to withdraw support is necessary to empty its pockets, pry open its fists, and silence its tongue. This is good not only for the oppressed but also for the oppressor who remains locked in the prison of their deception.

Others may say, "Well, it's going to take time, so we need

to be patient." Again, who usually says that? The people in power. Yes, healing does take time. But that's not what the immediate need is. Once the truth is established, those in the wrong must repent—must turn, must acknowledge their specific actions, must recognize the specific wounds caused, and must ask for forgiveness. And that can be done immediately without needing the approval of legal and public relations teams. The victims deserve, and therefore bystanders ought to demand, immediate truth seeking and truth telling. If leadership is governed by truth and not by deception, then they will seek and speak the truth no matter the cost, and if that cost entails lawsuits, falling attendance, or even shuttering the doors of the institution, then it is worth the cost, because the establishment of truth will always matter more than our establishments.

One example of this fearless truth seeking is a school I'll call "Monroe University." Monroe University wanted to discover how people of color on their campus were being treated. A few professors and students had individually brought up concerns through an anonymous survey that they didn't feel the university treated people of color with equity. Rather than file the concerns away as misguided or disruptive, the administration hired an outside independent organization to conduct a campus-wide assessment. There were no specific allegations of discrimination, and there was no public scandal, but the university was troubled that they might have a significant blind spot. The assessment team did a yearlong review of policies, survey responses, and interviews. The

If leadership is governed by truth, then they will seek and speak the truth no matter the cost, because the establishment of truth will always matter more than our establishments.

administration followed each of the recommendations that came out of the assessment. Nothing was buried. As a result, everyone at the university felt safe bringing their concerns to the administration. They knew they'd be taken seriously and have their voices heard.

A safe community gives people the freedom to say, "Something's not right." A safe community searches for understanding until what doesn't seem right is clearly identified, named, and described. A safe community addresses what isn't right, even if it means putting their own reputation on the line. And if the system itself isn't right, then a safe community will consider whether its presence is part of the problem. A safe community gives no room for the language of abuse to spread, because it keeps the lights on. In that light, truth moves freely. People do not keep their stories to themselves for fear of how others will respond. In a safe community, grooming is confronted before a person is victimized. In a safe community, truth telling increases as the strategies of deception are more easily spotted, first in ourselves and then in others.

Forgiveness and Advocacy

And I forgive you.

I could hardly believe I had just written those words. It was around 4 a.m. on Monday morning, February 15, 2016, and I was staring down at around seven pages covered with sentences that each began with the phrase "I was angry when . . ." I hadn't planned to write for most of the night. I simply wanted to do something with the question the senior pastor had asked me: "Where did this anger come from?" It was lodged in my soul like a deep splinter, and I could not ignore the throbbing pain it caused. Perhaps that was the point. So I decided to list each of the reasons I was angry. Injustice after injustice filled the pages. *I have every right to be angry*, I thought. *Everyone ought to be angry.* This practice of taking an inventory of wrongs was both validating and crushing. Something wasn't right. And grief and anger were a natural response to that realization.

I had no idea my list would end with the words, "And I forgive you." To be honest, I'm still trying to make sense of that response. That moment of forgiveness liberated me, not just from the hold another's wrongs had over me, but it liberated me to a place where I could oppose the abuse without the motive of personal revenge. The act of forgiveness didn't shut down my advocacy. Rather, it spun me back into the fray with a clearer mind and a strengthened resolve.

In some ways, this moment marked the beginning of a new stage in my efforts to combat evil. I'm still seeking answers to the mystery of forgiveness. I do know this: I would not have wanted someone to say to me, "Have you forgiven him yet?" I've encountered too many people who push forgiveness on others as a way of dealing with their own discomfort. For me, the choice to forgive was intensely personal, and its occurrence had a unique place in my unique story. I don't know if this will be true for you, but the path I took to forgiveness was lined with painful memories that were difficult to walk through. It would have been much easier to take the path that tramples the memories deep below ground, never to be surfaced. The act of telling and remembering somehow led me to an unexpected forgiveness. I've since come to believe it is better to remember and forgive than to forgive and forget.

A week after I wrote the words "And I forgive you," I informed the board that I would stay only if they hired a top-notch independent party to investigate my claims, that the entire board needed to be subject to investigation, and that they had one week to respond or I would resign immediately. My forgiveness did not call off my pursuit of truth. If anything, it accelerated it.

Whatever you are facing, I hope you can take the next step. People might try to tell you that the next and only step is to forgive and "move on." The next best step toward freedom and healing is the one that you choose. The next best sentence in your story is the one you write with your own pen. As your eyes are opened, you will see more clearly and will come to a deeper understanding of what happened to you. Only then will giving up the desire for revenge or a different past be done in a meaningful way. Only then will you know what you are forgiving if you make that choice, what you are seeking justice for if you pursue it, and what you are committed to preventing in the future.

CHAPTER 9 SUMMARY

WHAT NOW?

Healing from abuse will take time, as will the journey toward
creating the kind of community where abuse cannot grow and
fester. But there are things you can do in the meantime. The
principle of opposite action—of doing the opposite of what an
abuser desires from you—offers one way. There is reason for
hope for a safer life and community.

REFRAME

In order to break free from the power of abuse, you can reframe
what the abuser has attempted to dismantle. Rather than allowing
the abuser to define you or your surroundings, you can act, one
step at a time, to choose the opposite. When you know the tactics
abusers use, you can *confront* abuse.

CULTIVATE BEAUTY

Every act of abuse is an assault on beauty, so one of the best ways
to begin your healing journey is to cultivate beauty in yourself and
in your surroundings. Finding beauty in relationships and in nature
can be a good start.

ACKNOWLEDGMENTS

My wife, Sarita, has shared every moment and taken every step with me along the journey toward the completion of this book. Her wisdom, resilience, love, and fight for what is right and good can be found everywhere. She and our children fill my life with beauty and joy amid work that can be ugly and sorrowful at times.

Our parents, siblings, and closest friends provided support for us during a time when we needed it most. My grandparents—affectionately known as Mom-mom and Pop-pop—opened their home to us when we were suddenly without one. The year we spent among family members who loved us was a time of rest and healing. I could not have continued on this journey without their assistance.

Throughout the writing of this book, my mind often went to joy-filled memories shared with the young people I was privileged to serve, to truth-filled conversations with older friends who were kind enough to impart their experience and wisdom, to colleagues who made personal sacrifices to stand for what was right, and to seasoned educators who helped guide my early research efforts.

I continue to discover the illuminating words and actions of survivors, advocates, and experts who are shining a light on abuse and deception—some for decades. Their words have informed my own. More than that, I have been inspired by their courage and sacrificial love for others.

Lastly, I am grateful for Keely Boeving, who carefully represented my writing as a literary agent; for Jillian Schlossberg at Tyndale for believing in the vision for this book and guiding the process; for Jonathan Schindler's editing; for Jen Phelps's thoughtful cover design; and for the entire team at Tyndale for wanting to contribute to the work of making our world safer from abuse.

WHAT TO DO
IF SOMETHING'S
NOT RIGHT

Dear reader,

This book may have helped confirm what you already felt was true—something's not right about your situation. Or maybe you feel as if you are just now beginning to see patterns you didn't notice before. That can be unnerving, and even scary. Because this book is not meant to be a blueprint— every situation is different and presents challenges that are unique to you—I want to encourage you to get help from a professional. It's important that your story is told and heard by a competent and caring expert who can support you as you try to make sense of and journey through the pages of this chapter in your life. I am forever grateful to professional therapists who have helped me see what I couldn't see when I walked through their door. They helped me make decisions and take actions I didn't think were possible when I picked up the phone to schedule an appointment. The truths they shared helped set me free.

If you are a leader in an organizational setting and the climate tells you something's not right, I want to urge you to follow the truth wherever it leads. It is okay, and often necessary, to turn to outside help from experts who can show you what is true through an independent and objective process of assessment or investigation. You will be surprised at what might be unearthed when members of an organization feel the freedom to speak because the people asking the questions and the processes being followed do not contain the ingredients of intimidation. The truths they uncover will have the power to set your organization free from abuse.

With hope for a safer future,

Wade

RESOURCES
FOR
SURVIVORS

It's common to feel alone. Know that help is out there. Locating the help you need, however, is a process that might seem overwhelming and at times frustrating. I encourage you to begin by doing some research. Learn about the different types of abuse and the various approaches to therapy. Compile a list of local therapists and advocacy centers that specialize in helping those in abusive situations. Do some additional research to see if they are well reviewed and recommended by other professionals. Prepare a list of questions and contact them to get more information.

The list I've compiled in this appendix is by no means exhaustive. It is meant to provide possible starting points as you explore sources of support. Local advocacy centers, therapists, and attorneys are often the best places to look for in-person help. I encourage you to use the resources listed here to help you understand your situation so you can more easily find a person or an organization with the expertise and availability to offer you the individualized help you need.

I recognize that not all situations are captured in this list of resources, but I've tried to cover many common scenarios.

General Resources for Abuse and Trauma

GLOBAL TRAUMA RECOVERY INSTITUTE
(www.missio.edu/global-trauma-recovery-institute)
The Global Trauma Recovery Institute provides "high quality continuing educational resources, skills training, and case consultation for mental health clinicians, ministry leaders, and professionals interested in addressing the needs of psychosocial trauma victims in the United States and around the world."

DIANE LANGBERG, PhD (www.dianelangberg.com)
"Dr. Diane Langberg is a practicing psychologist whose clinical expertise includes 35 years of working with trauma survivors and clergy. She speaks internationally on topics related to women, trauma, ministry and the Christian life." Dr. Langberg has produced numerous books, articles, videos, and podcasts on the topics of trauma, abuse, narcissism, power, and recovery.

THE NATIONAL CHILD TRAUMATIC STRESS NETWORK
(www.nctsn.org)
The mission of the NCTSN is "to raise the standard of care and improve access to services for traumatized children, their families and communities throughout the United States."

RAPE, ABUSE & INCEST NATIONAL NETWORK (RAINN)

(www.rainn.org)

"RAINN (Rape, Abuse & Incest National Network) is the nation's largest anti-sexual violence organization. RAINN created and operates the National Sexual Assault Hotline (800.656.HOPE, online.rainn.org [and] rainn.org/es) in partnership with more than 1,000 local sexual assault service providers across the country and operates the DoD Safe Helpline for the Department of Defense. RAINN also carries out programs to prevent sexual violence, help survivors, and ensure that perpetrators are brought to justice."

NATIONAL SEXUAL VIOLENCE RESOURCE CENTER

(www.nsvrc.org)

"Every state and territory has an organization designated to coordinate the activities of rape crisis efforts and represent that state or territory as its coalition. NSVRC maintains a Directory of State and Territory Coalitions, as well as a Directory of Victim/Survivor Support Organizations that provide services to survivors."

BOOKS

- Herman, Judith. *Trauma and Recovery: The Aftermath of Violence—from Domestic Abuse to Political Terror.* New York: Basic Books, 2015.
- Langberg, Diane Mandt. *On the Threshold of Hope: Opening the Door to Healing for Survivors of Sexual Abuse.* Carol Stream, IL: Tyndale House, 1999.

- Salter, Anna C. *Predators: Pedophiles, Rapists, and Other Sex Offenders: Who They Are, How They Operate, and How We Can Protect Ourselves and Our Children.* New York: Basic Books, 2003.

Resources for Adult Survivors of Child Abuse

HELP FOR ADULT VICTIMS OF CHILD ABUSE
(www.havoca.org)
"HAVOCA is run by survivors for adult survivors of child abuse. We provide support, friendship and advice for any adult whose life has been affected by childhood abuse."

ADULT SURVIVORS OF CHILD ABUSE
(www.ascasupport.org)
"Adult Survivors of Child Abuse (ASCA) is an international self-help support group program designed specifically for adult survivors of neglect, physical, sexual, and/or emotional abuse."

BOOKS

- Bear, Euan. *Adults Molested as Children: A Survivor's Manual for Women and Men.* With Peter T. Dimock. Orwell, VT: Safer Society Press, 1988.
- Courtois, Christine A. *Adult Survivors of Child Sexual Abuse.* Milwaukee, WI: Families International, 1993.

Resources for Survivors of Clergy Sexual Abuse

SNAP—SURVIVORS NETWORK OF THOSE ABUSED BY PRIESTS (www.snapnetwork.org)

"SNAP is the largest, oldest and most active self-help group for clergy sex abuse victims, whether assaulted by ministers, priests, nuns or rabbis. SNAP is a confidential, safe place for wounded men and women to be heard, supported and healed. SNAP works tirelessly to achieve two goals: to heal the wounded and to protect the vulnerable. The organization has more than 25,000 members and support groups meet in over 60 cities across the U.S. and the world."

THE SILENT MAJORITY: ADULT VICTIMS OF SEXUAL EXPLOITATION BY CLERGY (www.adultsabusedbyclergy.org)

A website that provides information centered around a study of clergy sexual misconduct with adults conducted by Baylor University School of Social Work in 2009.

Resources for Male Survivors of Abuse

MALESURVIVOR (www.malesurvivor.org)

"For 25 years, MaleSurvivor has fostered a healing community where thousands of men from more than 190 countries come together to find support, information and—most importantly—hope. MaleSurvivor is dedicated to providing personalized support for men at every stage of the healing process. We facilitate dialogue among survivors, as well as between survivors and professional therapists, on our online forums like a vibrant and moderated discussion board, online 24/7 chat and at in-person events. We provide educational resources that help empower them to process their past and look forward to a brighter future."

1IN6 (www.1in6.org)

1in6 provides "information and services for men with histories of unwanted or abusive sexual experiences, and anyone who cares about them." Resources include a 24/7 online helpline, free and confidential online support groups, trauma-informed trainings and webinars, and male survivor stories.

Resources for Survivors of Domestic Violence

NATIONAL COALITION AGAINST DOMESTIC VIOLENCE (NCADV) (www.ncadv.org)

The NCADV mission "is to lead, mobilize and raise our voices to support efforts that demand a change of conditions that lead to domestic violence such as patriarchy, privilege, racism, sexism, and classism. We are dedicated to supporting survivors and holding offenders accountable and supporting advocates."

DOMESTIC SHELTERS (www.domesticshelters.org)

"We make finding the right shelter and information about domestic violence easier. Instead of searching the Internet, it is all right here. We've painstakingly verified information on shelters in LA to shelters in NY, and every domestic violence program in between. If you or a friend is suffering from physical abuse, emotional abuse, psychological abuse or verbal abuse, this free service can help. Select domestic violence programs based on location, service and language needs. Find 24-hour hotlines in your area, service listings, and helpful articles on domestic violence statistics, signs and cycles of abuse, housing services, emergency services, legal and financial services, support groups for women, children and families, and more."

NATIONAL DOMESTIC VIOLENCE HOTLINE
(www.thehotline.org)
A 24/7 free hotline with access to service providers and shelters throughout the United States.

NATIONAL NETWORK TO END DOMESTIC VIOLENCE
(www.nnedv.org)
"NNEDV represents the 56 state and U.S. territory coalitions against domestic violence. Domestic violence coalitions serve as state-wide and territory-wide leaders in the efforts to end domestic violence. These organizations connect local domestic violence service providers and are valuable resources for information about services, programs, legislation, and policies that support survivors of domestic violence."

Resources for Survivors of Incest

SURVIVORS OF INCEST ANONYMOUS (www.siawso.org)
"SIA, started in 1982, is a 12-Step, self-help recovery program modeled after Alcoholics Anonymous. SIA is for men and women, 18 years and older, who were sexually abused as children."

BOOKS

- Courtois, Christine A. *Healing the Incest Wound: Adult Survivors in Therapy.* New York: W. W. Norton, 1988.
- Herman, Judith Lewis. *Father-Daughter Incest.* Cambridge: Harvard University Press, 2000.

Resources for Survivors of Educator Sexual Abuse

STOP EDUCATOR SEXUAL ABUSE MISCONDUCT & EXPLOITATION (S.E.S.A.M.E.) (www.sesamenet.org)
"S.E.S.A.M.E. was founded in 1991 by volunteers who saw a need in their community. Today, the need for S.E.S.A.M.E. still persists, and a dedicated group of volunteer advocates and experts continue the work of the founders so that the nation's schools are safer for children."

Resources for Survivors of Organized Abuse

DR. MICHAEL SALTER (www.organisedabuse.com)
Dr. Michael Salter "specialises in the study of organised abuse and complex trauma." According to the website, "Organised

abuse involves multiple adults who conspire to sexually abuse one or more children. Organised abuse can include the sexual exchange of children between perpetrators as well as the manufacture of child abuse images and the prostitution of children for financial gain or other advantages."

Resources for Survivors of Elder Abuse or Disability Abuse

NATIONAL ADULT PROTECTIVE SERVICES ASSOCIATION (www.napsa-now.org)
"The National Adult Protective Services Association (NAPSA) is a national non-profit 501(c) (3) organization with members in all fifty states. Formed in 1989, the goal of NAPSA is to provide Adult Protective Services (APS) programs a forum for sharing information, solving problems, and improving the quality of services for victims of elder and vulnerable adult mistreatment."

VERA INSTITUTE OF JUSTICE (www.vera.org)
"People with disabilities are much more vulnerable to harm. They're three times more likely to be sexually abused as children, and three times more likely to be victims of violent crimes ranging from robbery to rape as adolescents and adults. As troubling, survivors rarely get the help they need to heal. Organizations dedicated to serving people with disabilities and Deaf people often have no experience working with victims of crime, while agencies focused on crime and victimization are typically ill-equipped to serve

people with differing abilities. Our work focuses on connecting professionals, breaking down systemic barriers to collaboration, and rigorously tracking performance—the only way to provide services that actually meet people's needs. Much of our work is focused on survivors of domestic and sexual violence." The Vera Institute of Justice manages the End Abuse of People with Disabilities website (www.endabusepwd.org).

Resources for Survivors of Abuse in Detention

JUST DETENTION INTERNATIONAL (www.justdetention.org) "JDI is a health and human rights organization that seeks to end sexual abuse in all forms of detention. Founded in 1980, JDI is the only organization in the U.S.—and the world—dedicated exclusively to ending sexual abuse behind bars. We hold government officials accountable for prisoner rape; challenge the attitudes and misperceptions that allow sexual abuse to flourish; and make sure that survivors get the help they need."

Resources for Survivors of Psychological Abuse

CONFUSION TO CLARITY (www.confusiontoclaritynow.com) A Christian resource that provides support and healing for women who have experienced covert narcissistic and psychological spousal abuse.

FLYING FREE (www.flyingfreenow.com)

Flying Free helps women "recover and heal from emotional and spiritual abuse while also discovering a life of freedom and joy in Christ."

BOOKS

- Hassan, Steven. *Combating Cult Mind Control: The #1 Best-Selling Guide to Protection, Rescue, and Recovery from Destructive Cults.* Rochester, VT: Park Street Press, 2015.
- Johnson, David, and Jeff VanVonderen. *The Subtle Power of Spiritual Abuse: Recognizing and Escaping Spiritual Manipulation and False Spiritual Authority within the Church.* Minneapolis: Bethany House, 2005.

Resources for Survivors of Workplace Abuse

END WORKPLACE ABUSE (www.endworkplaceabuse.com)

"Part of the National Workplace Bullying Coalition, a 501(c)3 nonprofit organization, we're a network of advocates from a variety of professional backgrounds and sectors working collaboratively to build a national movement to end workplace abuse. We believe in the urgency to make workplaces safe, healthy, and inclusive for everyone. We aim to raise awareness about the pervasive harms of workplace abuse, advocate for legislation that protects workers from abusive behaviors, build coalition and community with other grassroots efforts that align with our vision, explore and develop solutions and ideas, and make resources available to those impacted by workplace abuse, including those who've been directly targeted."

WORKPLACE BULLYING INSTITUTE
(www.workplacebullying.org)
"WBI is . . . dedicated to the eradication of workplace bullying that combines help for individuals, research, books, public education, training for professionals-unions-employers, legislative advocacy, and consulting solutions for organizations. Established 1997."

Resources for Survivors of Healthcare Provider Abuse

THERAPY EXPLOITATION LINK LINE (TELL)
(www.therapyabuse.org)
"TELL is a peer support network that seeks to help victims and survivors of exploitation by psychotherapists and other healthcare providers find the resources they will need to understand what has happened to them, to take action, and to heal."

Resources for Survivors of Dating Abuse

LOVE IS RESPECT (www.loveisrespect.org)
"Highly-trained advocates offer support, information and

advocacy to young people who have questions or concerns about their dating relationships. We also provide information and support to concerned friends and family members, teachers, counselors, service providers and members of law enforcement. Free and confidential phone, live chat and texting services are available 24/7/365."

BREAK THE CYCLE (www.breakthecycle.org)
"Break the Cycle inspires and supports young people 12–24 to build healthy relationships and create a culture without abuse. We are a culturally affirming organization that centers young people, caring adults, and communities in our prevention and intervention efforts. Our dynamic and diverse team believes that all young people deserve to live in a world where they can thrive."

Resources for Survivors of all Types of Crime

NATIONAL CENTER FOR VICTIMS OF CRIME (www.victimsofcrime.org)
"The National Center for Victims of Crime is a nonprofit organization that advocates for victims' rights, trains professionals who work with victims, and serves as a trusted source of information on victims' issues. After more than 25 years, we remain the most comprehensive national resource committed to advancing victims' rights and helping victims of crime rebuild their lives. The National Center is, at its core, an advocacy organization committed to—and working on

behalf of—crime victims and their families. Rather than focus the entire organization's work on one type of crime or victim, the National Center addresses all types of crime."

Resources for Suicide Prevention

NATIONAL SUICIDE PREVENTION LIFELINE
(www.suicidepreventionlifeline.org)
"The Lifeline provides 24/7, free and confidential support for people in distress, prevention and crisis resources for you or your loved ones, and best practices for professionals."

RESOURCES
FOR
ADVOCATES

For faith-based organizational assessments, independent investigations, and safeguarding certifications in the United States, I recommend Godly Response to Abuse in the Christian Environment (GRACE) (www.netgrace.org).

THIRTYONE:EIGHT (www.thirtyoneeight.org)—United Kingdom
"An independent Christian charity which helps individuals, organisations, charities, faith and community groups to protect vulnerable people from abuse. Our vision is a world where every child and adult can feel, and be, safe, and to achieve this vision we work together with a network of thousands of organisations across the UK helping them to create safer places."

CHUCK DEGROAT, author of *When Narcissism Comes to Church: Healing Your Community from Emotional and Spiritual Abuse* (www.chuckdegroat.net)
"Chuck is Professor of Counseling and Christian Spirituality at Western Theological Seminary, Holland, MI, and Co-Founder

and a Senior Fellow at Newbigin House of Studies, San Francisco. He is a licensed therapist, author, retreat leader, and spiritual director."

ACADEMY ON VIOLENCE & ABUSE (www.avahealth.org)
"The mission of the AVA is to advance health education and research on the recognition, treatment, and prevention of the health effects of violence and abuse throughout the lifecourse."

JOYFUL HEART FOUNDATION (www.joyfulheartfoundation.org)
"Founded in 2004, Joyful Heart is a leading national organization with a mission to transform society's response to sexual assault, domestic violence, and child abuse, support survivors' healing, and end this violence forever. Joyful Heart carries out its mission through an integrated program portfolio of education and advocacy. Our work is paving the way for innovative approaches to treating trauma; igniting shifts in the way the public views and responds to sexual assault, domestic violence, and child abuse; and reforming and advancing policies and legislation to ensure access to justice for survivors."

AMERICAN PROFESSIONAL SOCIETY ON THE ABUSE OF CHILDREN (www.apsac.org)
"As a multidisciplinary group of professionals, APSAC achieves its mission in a number of ways; most notably through expert training and educational activities, policy leadership and collaboration, and consultation that emphasize theoretically sound, evidence-based principles."

ZERO ABUSE PROJECT
(www.zeroabuseproject.org)

The mission of the Zero Abuse Project is "to protect children from abuse and sexual assault, by engaging people and resources through a trauma-informed approach of education, research, advocacy, and advanced technology."

SAFE COMMUNITIES (www.safecommunitiespa.org)

An organization that helps "youth programs, schools, faith congregations, and other community organizations to develop institutional policies and cultures that can prevent child sexual abuse; educate adults about how to keep kids safe; and spread models that enable adult survivors to heal and lead in uniting communities to end child sexual abuse."

ACES CONNECTION (www.acesconnection.com)

ACEs Connection "connects those who are implementing trauma-informed and resilience-building practices based on ACEs science. The network's 40,000+ members share their best practices, while inspiring each other to grow the ACEs movement."

NATIONAL CHILDREN'S ADVOCACY CENTER
(www.nationalcac.org)

"The NCAC models, promotes, and delivers excellence in child abuse response and prevention through service, education, and leadership."

CHILD ADVOCACY CENTRES/CHILD & YOUTH ADVOCACY CENTRES (www.cac-cae.ca)

There are hundreds of child advocacy centers throughout the United States and in more than 20 countries. "Child Advocacy Centres/Child & Youth Advocacy Centres (CACs/CYACs) provide a co-ordinated, multidisciplinary approach in a safe, comfortable environment to address the needs of children, youth and their families."

DARKNESS TO LIGHT (www.d2l.org)

"Through the combination of research, education, and community advocacy, Darkness to Light uses a social behavior change approach to pioneer new training initiatives that bring child sexual abuse to the attention of the broader cultural conversation. Over the years, nearly two million adults in 76 countries have been trained to protect children through the efforts of more than 12,000 Certified Instructors and Authorized Facilitators."

STOP IT NOW! (www.stopitnow.org)

"Stop It Now! prevents the sexual abuse of children by mobilizing adults, families and communities to take actions that protect children before they are harmed. We provide support, information and resources to keep children safe and create healthier communities. Since 1992, we have identified, refined and shared effective ways for individuals, families and communities to act to prevent child sexual abuse before children are harmed—and to get help for everyone involved."

#SETTHEEXPECTATION (www.settheexpectation.org)

A nonprofit "dedicated to combating sexual and physical violence through raising awareness, giving back, education and direct engagement with coaches, young men and boys in high school, collegiate and professional athletic programs."

CENTRE FOR RESEARCH & EDUCATION ON VIOLENCE AGAINST WOMEN & CHILDREN (www.learningtoendabuse.ca)

The Centre's mission statement reads, "We facilitate the collaboration of individuals, groups and institutions representing the diversity of the community to pursue research questions and training opportunities to understand and prevent violence and abuse. We serve local, national and international communities by producing useful information and tools to assist in the daily work to prevent and stop violence towards women and children and vulnerable adults."

ADVOCATEWEB (www.advocateweb.org)

"AdvocateWeb is a nonprofit organization providing information and resources to promote awareness and understanding of the issues involved in the exploitation of persons by trusted helping professionals. We are attempting to be a helpful resource for victims/survivors, their family and friends, the general public, and for victim advocates and professionals."

ECPAT (www.ecpat.org)

"ECPAT is the only child rights organisation that is solely focusing on ending the sexual exploitation of children.

Today, we are a growing network of over 110 civil society organisations in over 100 countries. Together we advocate for a stronger legal environment to protect children; we raise awareness among the public about the issue; we partner with the private sector to prevent their services of being misused; we research to better understand this crime and we help survivors and victims to come to terms with what has happened to them—and better understand their rights."

NOTES

CHAPTER 1: THE SHOW MUST GO ON
1. References to Goffman's work throughout this chapter refer to Erving Goffman, *The Presentation of Self in Everyday Life* (New York: Anchor Books, 2008).

CHAPTER 2: CHARMS
1. *Leaving Neverland*, directed by Dan Reed (New York: HBO, 2019).
2. *Surviving R. Kelly*, six-part series directed and written by Nigel Bellis and Astral Finnie, Bunim/Murray Productions and Kreativ Inc. (New York: Lifetime Network, 2019).
3. See Erving Goffman, *The Presentation of Self in Everyday Life* (New York: Anchor Books, 2008).

CHAPTER 3: DISMANTLING YOUR INTERNAL WORLD
1. Diane Langberg, "Trauma in the Family," 2019 Global Community of Practice (COP) Global Gathering, March 12, 2019, 49:20, https://www.youtube.com/watch?v=ilGIROL455A.

CHAPTER 5: THE SILENT STRUGGLE
1. Julie Roys, "Hard Times at Harvest," *World*, December 13, 2018, https://world.wng.org/2018/12/hard_times_at_harvest.

CHAPTER 6: ON THE DEFENSE
1. Micah 2:11.
2. Elizabeth Heyrick, *Immediate, Not Gradual Abolition: Or, an Inquiry into the Shortest, Safest, and Most Effectual Means of Getting Rid of West Indian Slavery* (Boston: Isaac Knapp, 1838), 27.

3. Alex Early, "MLK on the Good Samaritan," *P. A. Early* (blog), September 13, 2017, http://paearly.com/blog/2017/9/13/mlk-on-the-good-samaritan.
4. Genesis 3:11-13.
5. Judith Herman, *Trauma and Recovery: The Aftermath of Violence—From Domestic Abuse to Political Terror* (New York: Basic Books, 2015), 8.

CHAPTER 7: CONCESSIONS
1. Elizabeth Heyrick, *Immediate, Not Gradual Abolition: Or, an Inquiry into the Shortest, Safest, and Most Effectual Means of Getting Rid of West Indian Slavery* (Boston: Isaac Knapp, 1838), 23.
2. This is a composite statement based on many that I've run across in my research.
3. Primo Levi, "Primo Levi's Heartbreaking, Heroic Answers to the Most Common Questions He Was Asked about 'Survival in Auschwitz,'" *New Republic*, February 17, 1986, https://newrepublic.com/article/119959/interview-primo-levi-survival-auschwitz.

CHAPTER 9: WHAT NOW?
1. Judith Herman, *Trauma and Recovery: The Aftermath of Violence—From Domestic Abuse to Political Terror* (New York: Basic Books, 2015), 7–8.
2. Elie Wiesel, "Nobel Prize Acceptance Speech" (Oslo City Hall, Norway, December 10, 1986), https://eliewieselfoundation.org/elie-wiesel/nobel prizespeech/.
3. Elizabeth Heyrick, *Immediate, Not Gradual Abolition: Or, an Inquiry into the Shortest, Safest, and Most Effectual Means of Getting Rid of West Indian Slavery* (Boston: Isaac Knapp, 1838), 4–5.

DISCUSSION
GUIDE

1. Wade defines abuse as whenever "someone treats
   you as an object they are willing to harm for their
   own benefit." Up to this point, what has been your
   definition of "abuse"? How does this description
   change your understanding of either your own
   experiences or the experiences of your loved
   ones?

2. Have you ever had an experience with an individual
   or organization that didn't feel *right*, that would
   be considered abusive in some form? How did
   that experience affect you physically, mentally,
   emotionally, and spiritually?

3. Wade suggests that, to a degree, we all use impression
   management tactics in our everyday interactions. Can
   you think of a recent instance of this in your own life?
   Why did you do this, and what was the result?

4. Like many charms, flattery isn't inherently an indicator of abuse. When have you experienced harmless flattery—and when has flattery been used as a predicator of harm?

5. What are some ways we can protect one another's identity and agency in our community so that it is more difficult for abusers to dismantle?

6. In your experience with survivors, what has been the biggest reason that they didn't share or report their abuse?

7. What makes a person or community a safe space for survivors to share their stories or report abuse? How can you contribute to this kind of space in your own community?

8. In chapter 7, Wade provides a helpful template for an authentic apology: the SCORE card. Which apology "letters" do you have the most trouble with in your own life? What is one way you can work to improve this the next time you have to apologize?

9. After abuse is exposed, the abusive individual or organization will likely try to demonstrate their goodness or how they've changed since the abuse occurred. In your experience, what makes the difference between an authentic change and one that's done simply to win back favor?

10. If you've been in an abusive situation or community, what does recovery look like for you? What is one step you can take toward healing today?

11. Wade asserts that learning to cultivate beauty is a great resource in the journey to healing. Is there anything beautiful in your life right now? What beauty are you hoping to see in your future?

ABOUT THE AUTHOR

WADE MULLEN is a researcher, assistant professor, author, and speaker. One of the reasons his writing and teaching resonates with many is because he knows the territory of abuse from personal experience and can identify with those who are walking or have walked a similar path. His work brings affirmation and enlightenment and is backed by the credibility of thorough research and careful analysis.

Wade is the director of the Master of Divinity Program at Capital Seminary & Graduate School, a division of Lancaster Bible College in Pennsylvania. He teaches both ministry and leadership courses and engages in ongoing research in the field of leadership. He also conducts assessments and provides consultation to organizations seeking to make their environments safer.

Wade earned his PhD in leadership studies from Capital Seminary & Graduate School. Additional education includes a master's in ministry with a concentration in leadership studies from Capital Seminary & Graduate School and a bachelor's in pre-seminary from Cairn University.

Wade and his wife, Sarita, live in Lancaster County, Pennsylvania, with their four children. Together they have been partners in the struggle to speak truth, promote good, and support those in need.